XANGANS

Graham Worthington and Other Xangans

XANGANS

Stories, Poems and Blogs from the World's Greatest Blogging Community

Angry Orchid Productions

ISBN: 1452868603

Cover design by methodElevated

Books by some of these authors are available through online retailers

By John Lindensmith

Mystery Man

By Graham Worthington

Wake of the Raven

Zorn: a Legend of the Days to Come

By Liz Zelvin

Death Will Help You Leave Him

Death Will Get You Sober

Dedicated

to

the Xangan Community

methodElevated

Stefanie Roszkowski, our cover designer

Stefanie is a freelance artist who lives near Detroit, MI. She enjoys drawing portraits of Xangans to hone her skills. She is passionate about illustration, graphic design, jewelry design and photography, as well as living an active, healthy lifestyle. As the lead artist and art director of a game development team, she spends much of her time creating concept art.

Contents

Contents

Contents

First, a foreword from the one and only....

TheTheologiansCafe

Dan

Dan, a tireless supporter of Xanga, has from his virtual café been one of the best known and most popular bloggers on Xanga for many years, provoking us to thought and laughter by his sometimes hilarious, sometimes serious questions.

Xanga....

.... has a special place in the hearts of all those who have come across the website. It is different from the other websites in that it mixes the thoughts and emotions of all those involved. I think every member of the Xanga community can look back over the years of posting and remember the ups and the downs of their lives. Some fought depression. Others mourned the death of a mother or the loss of a child. And yet others were just practicing their writing skills in order to one-day move into the professional writing business. We came together to share our pain, addictions and struggles with someone that would read them.

So many days, I cried while reading a post only to find myself laughing and celebrating with the next entry I read.

I appreciate Graham putting this book together as a lasting memory of those day-to-day entries. He showed his dedication to the Xanga community with a tireless effort of looking through the posts, taking the submissions and turning it into what you are reading here today.

By Dan, TheTheologiansCafe

Darkoozeripple

Graham Worthington

I was born in England, in the North of great industrial towns, separated by vast expanses of hills and moors, the land of *Wuthering Heights,* where I wrote my first story at age eleven. As I approached publishing my first novel, I joined Xanga to do research for my second. Out of fascination, I remained a Xangan.

Editor's Introduction

I first joined Xanga in 2006. Like many Xangans, I flirted with other blogging systems, many of greater size, yet they did not touch my heart in the same way, for their impersonality made them irrelevant. To me, Xanga remains the only one in which the written word rules, and genuine exchanges of ideas and feelings occurs.

Here, on Xanga, I find a true window into the virtual world that has become the new dimension of this new century. Here I learn how people think today in a wide variety of cultures, and I met writers as real people. Here I meet face to face with my neighbors in this world without the filter of media bias.

Here the young and idealistic mix with the older and seasoned, the cynical wrestle with the devout, and light-hearted humor alternates with angry examination of our troubled world's problems.

Organising this collection into book format has been both a learning and a humbling experience to me. I have had to lay aside many of my opinions as to what is relevant in life and what is not, and go with what the real people on Xanga value in their lives, and this has helped me to expand the limitations of my own too-narrow personality. As I juggled the order of the pieces I'd received, as I pondered over fonts and headers, people who I saw only as interested authors became real to me as never before, and I am touched by the trust they have placed in me, and hope I have presented their humanity well.

All stories, all poems, all essays, all plays, all films begin as thoughts. The great talent and complexity of the human mind, its power to know, to discover, to invent, to just plain figure things out; these lie dreaming, unknown, uncrystallised, unexpressed until they find an outlet. Xanga is that outlet.

By Graham Worthington, darkoozeripple

The_Church_of_Fat

John Lindensmith

John R. Lindensmith is a 21-year-old writer from Mandan, North Dakota. He was born in Japan, where his parents served as missionaries. In 2006, he self-published and promoted a psychological thriller entitled *Mystery Man*, which is available through online retailers.

Another Night on the Town

John Lindensmith

Another night on the town. Just girls and booze and lots of smoking and driving fast and people laughing like idiots thinking they're so goddamn cool but really they're just like everybody else. I'm sitting in the back of the car and we're moving forty miles too fast in a twenty-five and the fat guy who is driving is smoking a Camel and he's on top of the whole world, thinking he's God, as the wheels seem to float off the ground as we reach 100 on the sixty and I'm staring out the window---feeling lost and empty---tracing my name on the fogged up glass, realizing I want to cry, but I'm so dead inside that I can't. My "friend" James turns to me and he asks me if I want a smoke and I say sure because I can't say no and I light up and I choke but then I ease into it, and every time I talk, I riddle my speech with "shits" and "fucks," (*because) I'm a shy weak fuck.

Just another night on the town. We're driving on Main, and there's all these empty souls just like us, standing around, chatting, lighting cigarettes, talking about how much they hate their parents, how much police officers suck, who they've fucked lately, what drugs they've tried--- some new drug I've never heard of. Collie parks the car on the curb and we crawl out and head toward this small gathering of blondes who are wearing bunny ears and smoking cigs and cussing and one girl has a beer bottle in her hand and they have really glossy eyes and lips and I feel sick.

"What's up?" one of the girls asks, and I'm not sure which one, because they all look the same.

"Just hanging out and shit," Collie says, and it seems we end every sentence with "and shit."

What you doin'?

Hangin' at the mall *and shit.*

Goin' to the movies *and shit.*
Just doing shit *and shit.*
And shit.
James is talking to me but I can't hear him and this car with a loud muffler rattles by and I hear screaming and these sophomores stick their heads out the car and flip everyone off and smoke cigs and scream "SUCK IT!" and we all force dead laughter and James says something again, something about milf chicks, but I'm not sure, because I'm on lots of Demerol and Lexapro and it seems like everyone I know is on Lexapro, and Lexapro makes it so you can't get it up, and I haven't had an orgasm for three months now and I really don't care.

One of the blonde chicks is talking to me and I take a drag off a cig and I pretend to listen.

"I'm thinking about getting a tattoo on my lower back. I'm like addicted to tattoos. It's like crack for me I just want to get more and more and I love it when people notice them and compliment them and"

blah blah blah fucking blah

"Um...yeah...sure...whatever," I say.

Collie is with some other blonde chick and they're talking and he leaves with her and James is off somewhere else, in the dark, smoking pot with some junkie most likely and I'm just standing here with this plastic girl wearing bunny ears, thinking she's the goddamn Playboy bunny or something. She even has a Playboy bunny tattoo on her neck.

God I want to kill her.

Her eyes are glossy and stuck in this permanent dumb ass stare and she just keeps talking about tattoos and I look around and I'm bored out of my fucking mind *and shit.*

She tells me she has a tattoo on her cunt. "Do you wanna fuck?" she asks, and I just shrug, and say, "Um...yeah...sure...whatever." I'm in her car and I'm fiddling with my fingers and listening to *Dashboard Confessional* and heavy-metal and rap on the stereo. A song plays "we're losing our souls" and tears run down my face and I wipe them away and the blonde cunt asks me what's wrong and I say, "Nothing. Just drive. Keep your goddamn eyes on the road."

She drives out to the middle of nowhere, in some field, and I look at her pasty face in the dark, smeared in gallons of cheap make-up, and she reeks of perfume and hand lotion. She starts taking off her shirt and asks me to rip off her pants and I tell her to take off her own goddamn clothes and just continue taking drags off my cigarette. She has ugly flap-jack boobs.

Eventually we're in the backseat and I can't get it up and I'm getting pissed off and the next thing I know I'm putting cigarettes out in her eyeballs and she's screaming and I punch her until she stops moving and breathing.

I remember the time I set my "friend" up with a girl who I knew was infected with herpes.

I remember the time I poked holes into my "friend's" condoms.

I remember the time I rolled cyanide into a "friend's" joint.

I remember the time I hung a stupid blonde in my shower and ate her out while she choked to death.

I'm sitting in some random restaurant with "the guys" and all we talk about is perverted sex and cars and girls and drugs and I stifle a yawn. The waiter is slow. I'm bored. I want to kill myself. James is talking about a girl he fucked tonight. He's saying she was easy pussy or something and I tell them I killed a girl tonight and there's this long awkward silence and then I force a smile and the whole table eases into nervous laughter.

My food is cold and I'm not hungry.

James talks about a new way of getting high. Collie talks about this girl he fucked with huge tits, but her cunt smelled like rotten tuna. Someone, I don't know who, talks about his parole officer and detention and how teachers are stupid and cops are stupid and parents are stupid and how authority is stupid and I'm just staring blank eyed at whichever longhair prick is spewing this dribble and I am so fucking sick. I have a slight feeling of déjà vu and realize its just history repeating itself.

Just another night on the town.

Collie says he once fucked a religious chick and made her cry out Jesus' name in bed and then someone, from somewhere, says, "We're all going to hell."

"Yeah, but we'll party!" Collie laughs.

My stomach is twisting up in knots. "Who fucking cares."

"What do you mean?"

"Who fucking cares," I say. "You go wherever...and...that's life. And shit."

"Yeah."

I take a sip of a soda, but my taste buds are so dull I can't tell what it is.

My cell rings and I pick it up and listen to some girl I don't know drone on the other end about how we never hang out anymore and that she's mad because I'm hanging out with James and she doesn't like James and I ask why and she doesn't tell me and I say, "Um...yeah...sure...whatever" and hang up on her and then I go into the bathroom and smash a toilet seat.

Next thing I know it's nearly one in the fucking morning and I'm at some party with a bunch of people I could care less about and I'm sipping spiked punch and these blonde girls are talking to me and they're wearing bunny ears.

"Did you know that Lilly is going out with Drake?"

I feel myself twitching and I say so very numbly I don't think anyone hears me, "Who cares."

I remember the time I got drunk at a party and I started screaming at everyone: "I'M GOING TO KILL YOU ALL! I FUCKING HATE ALL OF YOU! YOU ALL THINK YOU'RE SO GODDAMN COOL! BUT YOU'RE FUCKING NOT!!! I WILL KILL YOU ALL! YOU WORTHLESS PIECES OF SHIT!!! YOU FUCKING GAY ASSHOLES!!!"

Everyone laughed. They said I was a fun drunk.

I listen to this guy talk about all the people he wants to kill. He wants to kill people who don't drink or smoke. He wants to kill people who believe in God. He wants to kill anyone who's a virgin. He wants to kill people who go to church. He wants to kill people who get good grades in school.

I tell him he's a fucking piece of shit.

He lunges at me but some blonde holds him back and I tell him I'm just fucking with him and I go grab him a glass of punch. I drop a cyanide tablet in it.

I'm trying to fingerbang some girl but her pussy is too tight and I can't get my fingers in. And I'm thinking I'll probably tell some longhair in study hall that she smells bad down there and she's too tight. And this makes me even more depressed and homicidal.

A girl shares a poem she wrote with me:
I see your eyes bleeding
I see your heart beating
I see everything that's wrong with you
and more
I see that you're a whore
I tell her it sucks and to shoot herself.

Someone asks me who I'm going out with and I actually say "your mom."

I look at the other guys at the party and they all have long hair and they're laughing like junkies and I'm just sitting in a corner, trying to be ignored, and I keep drinking punch, and I feel woozy.

I get bored of the stupid repetitive sex jokes and the drama shit and guys kicking around soda cans for amusement and....

I leave and go to another party, in the next room, but I can't tell the difference.

James comes up to me, and I think I already know what he's going to say. He's going to ask me if I know someone. Most conversations here start with "Do you know (insert name)?" And then it's followed by a less amusing story about said person or perhaps some stupid rumor or some drama shit that I really don't give a fuck about.

Two blondes are bitching about who slept with a certain guy and I am not feeling good.

"Hey, do you know that one Miller girl?" James asks.

"There's a million fucking Millers."

"Uh...she's the blonde one."

"Who cares."

"Yeah. Who cares."

Long silence.

"Who fucking cares," I say again.

"Uh...yeah...I don't know."

"Uh...yeah...I dunno," I mock.

Blah blah blah *and shit.*

There's a long silence, and then James says, "I don't know what I'm gonna do with my life, man." And since the topic of conversation isn't perverted sex or girls or cars or drugs, I have no idea what to say, and I get nervous, and start fidgeting, lighting a cigarette, and and and and....

"Uh...yeah...sure...whatever," I say, walking off into the crowd.

Just another night on the town. And shit.

Alyxandri

Cynthia Craig

I'm a student majoring in English Literature at the University of South Florida in Tampa, FL

Last Night in My Dream

Alyxandri

Last night in my dream you had no voice

but the voice that I read

on napkins like stone tablets

And I knew that you were a religious experience

or as close to one that could appear

to a lonely atheist.

And darling, I believe in you

And I believe in me

Believe in love, in its misery,

in its power to save and its

strength to destroy.

And if he reached out a hand,

told me to have faith,

I am sure that I would drown

beneath the waves

of the Galilee, with my mustard
seed

clasped tightly within my fist.

But I believe in me,

and I believe in you.

I believe in love

and I guess God too

but only in my sleep.

Lost-In-Reverie

Jessica Buckridge

Jessica has been blogging on Xanga since 2002. She holds a Bachelor of Arts degree from Hunter College, where she studied music. She also has a passion for art and literature, and a great love of travel. She aspires to add something beautiful to the world.

Because I Want to Believe; Or, Why I Am Sometimes Jealous of People with Faith

Lost-in-Reverie

Any seriously religious subscribers I have are all going to dive for the "unsubscribe" button after reading this post.

A bit of backstory before I truly begin: I was raised Catholic. I attended church, and catechism classes every week for pretty much as long as I can remember, up until I was confirmed at age 14. For a time, I assumed everyone else in the world was also Catholic. Then I went to school, and met one of my earliest best friends who was Jewish. We shared our religious traditions with each other (well, as much as you can at age 7, anyway) and I first started to question my belief. I remember going home one day and asking someone, probably my mother, "But if Jewish people believe this, and Catholic people believe this, who is right?" It was a few more years before it dawned on me that not only was everyone else in the world not necessarily Catholic, the concept of religion extended far beyond the ideas of being Christian or Jewish. I was about 10 years old when I first started reading about other religions, and realizing that I no longer believed in my own.

Now that I've gotten that out of the way....

What is religion anyway? It's not the easiest thing to define. What makes a religion a religion? A professor of mine, in teaching my Puerto Rican History class, recently said something during a lecture that struck me. We were discussing a variety of religions, Catholicism, Protestantism, Buddhism, Taoism, Confucianism, etc. He said that religions that do not have a god are not religions. I very much disagree with his claim. While a god or gods may be a central part of many religious traditions, I do not believe they are a make-or-break factor. I think that religion and philosophy are very closely related, and that many belief systems - Taoism, for example, comes to mind - can be considered both, not just one or the other.

So, back to the original question, the definition of religion. My first instinct when writing this entry was to run over to Merriam Webster's site and see what they had to say. Unfortunately, their definition suffers very much from the common problem of defining a word with itself. I turned instead to good old Dictionary.com for a definition I prefer:

"Religion - a set of beliefs concerning the cause, nature, and purpose of the universe, esp. when considered as the creation of a superhuman agency or agencies, usually involving devotional and ritual observances, and often containing a moral code governing the conduct of human affairs."

Okay, so now you have some idea of the concept I'm thinking of when I think "religion," I'm thinking large scale - Eastern religion, Western religion, monotheistic, polytheistic, all that good stuff.

I have been interested in religions pretty much since I realized I didn't believe in mine anymore. I don't know exactly what it was that finally disintegrated my faith, and belief in god. Maybe it was when I found out the truth behind the Bible, and who had written it, and when, and who had revised and edited it over the years. Maybe it was when I found out that people had been waiting for 2,000 years for the supposed return of some messiah, and he still wasn't here yet. Maybe it was when every single time I'd pray and talk up to the sky, there was never any answer to be had. All I know is, I got to a point when it dawned on me that, in my eyes, my religion was nothing more than a nifty bedtime story someone made up thousands of years ago to make sense of something that they didn't understand, and to comfort them in times of hardship. When I was about 10, and started reading about other religions, I began to find all sorts of religions, beliefs, and traditions that interested me. From the time I was 10 until the time I was about 15 or 16 I'd guess, I had "converted" probably about a dozen times. I was constantly looking for something, and in every new religion I'd read about, I'd think that I'd found it. From Paganism, to Buddhism, to Wicca, to Judaism, to Hinduism, to Taoism, even back to Catholicism from time to time. I'd think that I'd found some mighty answer. But I never did. I learned many things. I incorporated many new philosophies into my lifestyle. But I could never find any faith.

And finally, many paragraphs later, we reach the conflict that the title implied. For those of you who are wondering why I chose such a title, I promise, I'm getting there. In my religion class, entitled "Religious Ideas In Modern Literature," we are reading a novel called <u>Barabbas</u>, by Par Lagerkvist, and as those of you who know your Bible may have guessed, it's about the man who was freed instead of Jesus at the time of the crucifixion. There's no real historical basis for the character, but I found the book to be incredibly moving, and perhaps it is because I could relate so much to Barabbas' character. There is a scene in which Barabbas, who has become a slave in the Roman empire, is brought before a governor with a fellow slave because they have both carved the name "Christos Iesus" on the back of their slave disks, the pendants they wear with the stamp of the state showing that they belong to the state. The governor asks the other slave about the inscription, and he says it is there because he is not a slave to the state, but rather that he belongs to his god. The governor then turns to Barabbas, and asks him if he believes in this same god. Barabbas is silent, and finally replies by saying "I have no god." The governor is confused, and asks why he wears the disk with the name carved in it. Barabbas replies "Because I want to believe."

"Because I want to believe." I don't consider myself part of any religion right now. This doesn't mean I'm an amoral heathen who is bereft of ethics. It doesn't mean I have no soul, as my mother once told me in the midst of a heated argument on the subject. It doesn't mean that I have no purpose in life, or any lack of motivation to do what is right. I wish sometimes that I could find the comfort of believing in something. I wish I had faith in some higher power, because I see it bring such comfort to so many people. I want to have that security blanket of truly believing that there's some god up there who will make it all turn out right in the end, or some universal energy that will put things in balance. I do everything that I can do to make myself a better person, but at the end of the day, the only thing I can believe in, and the only thing I can truly have faith in is myself, and the power that lies within me. And sometimes, I'm jealous of people who can believe in something more.

Are you a religious person? Do you have faith? Do you believe in god? What god? Why do you believe in whatever god you believe in? If you don't believe in god, why not? Do you wish you did?

Reading Lolita

By Alyxandri

Alexis lounges on the floor of P's apartment, reading *Lolita*. P cooks in the kitchen- some kind of potato and cheese dish. They are both engaged in their separate tasks and do not talk much except for the occasional comment.

"How is the book?" P calls from the kitchen.

"Really good. Want to hear the plot?"

"Sure, ok."

"It's about this guy who is into little girls- nine to fourteen-year-olds," Alexis talks in a bored voice without raising her eyes from the book. "He falls in love with a young girl, Lolita, and marries her mom so that he can get at her."

"Holy shit," laughs P. "That's fucked up."

"Yeah. It's written from the perspective of the pedophile so you kind of start to sympathize with him. You start to want what he wants."

"What, little girls?" P laughs again. "I already have one." P is six years older than Alexis.

P ducks out of the kitchen, smiling suggestively. P and Alexis look at each other for a fraction of a moment. The book is thrown aside.

First the t-shirts are pulled off. It is a mutual effort on the carpet of the barren living room. P playfully pushes Alexis onto the floor. He unzips her jeans and pulls them down about her ankles. Much slower, he pulls back her white cotton underwear. He does it with an attitude of reverence- the reverent wonder of a child unwrapping a much-anticipated Christmas gift.

Alexis arches her back obediently as P reaches a hand under her to unlatch her bra. First try, second try, third is the charm. Alexis lies quietly on her back in a state of sublime lustful calm as P lowers his mouth to her exposed flesh. P's breath travels up the insides of her thighs. Tongue darts in and out. Alexis moans a bit, mostly from pleasure but partly as encouragement.

After a few minutes of this, Alexis sits up and energetically pushes P backwards by pressing her small hands against his chest. He is now in a kneeling position over her. She unzips his shorts in a deft movement and abruptly yanks them down. Then, ducking her head downward, she starts to pay back his favor. While she works, Alexis pulls at the muscles in P's lower back, massaging them roughly.

Alexis stops. "Isn't M going to be home soon?"

"I don't know. Maybe." P shrugs. P is giving Alexis that peculiar look of his. Wide, twinkling eyes staring at her without blinking. Large smile, a full set of teeth showing. A mental picture of a wolf on the hunt bursts into Alexis' mind.

"Let's take this to your room. I'm not much of an exhibitionist."

Alexis strolls naked through the hallway and into the dark of P's room with an aura of deliberateness. Without looking at P, she walks up to his one bedroom window. A streetlight outside illuminates her face and the front of her body in a dusky orange glow. Alexis bends over, still not looking at P. She arches her back and pushes her hands against the windowsill. She looks over her shoulder with an expectant smile.

P is a good deal taller than Alexis which makes sex difficult while standing. But P eventually slips into Alexis, grabs her hips and pulls. Alexis pushes against the windowsill with her hands. Their bodies slam together. Their faces are hidden from each other. They are bodies in motion, bodies only. Alexis sees a playground outside the window. Alexis moans with pleasure. She hears laughter coming from outside, but no one is there.

Alexis stands upright while P is still inside of her and rocks back and forth against him. P gasps. His hands wander from her nipples to her stomach to her clit. The hands go up and down. The bodies rock back and forth. Alexis is thrown against the wall.

Next, Alexis has P on the floor. She is on top. She is leaning forward to bite his neck and chest, leaning backwards and holding his thighs. P's hands run over every inch of her body- stomach, thighs, boobs, buttocks. Alexis is always vaguely aroused and surprised at P's treatment of her body. Much in the same way a mother feels about her baby, P finds no part of her body off-limits or disgusting. Every piece of her flesh is a tool for stimulation.

Now, P is on top. Alexis clings to him like a child and whispers that she loves it when he slides in and out of her. P slides in and out with increasing speed. Alexis emits a dramatic porn star moan, and P immediately comes.

Alexis masturbates and orgasms in about two minutes. P lies on her, resting his head on a boob. He closes his eyes.

He reminds Alexis of a young child seeking comfort from a parent. Alexis wonders if sex is a bandage- a bandage for all of the broken little boys who grow up into men. Broken little boys whose fathers abused them, whose mothers abandoned them. So much tragedy inside of every man. No one is whole anymore. Everyone seeks pleasure, but is driven by comfort.

"That was good," Alexis says.

"That was very good," P replies with a smile. His eyes are still closed, his head resting against Alexis.

"*Exceptionally* good," Alexis smiles too.

P suddenly raises himself over Alexis, covering her body. He is close, so close. Close in a different way. He stares into her eyes intently.

"I really like you," he says.

"I really like you too," Alexis says back. She blankly stares at his face, which is glowing orange in the darkness.

P kisses her stomach, slowly pressing his lips against her skin. He looks into her eyes again with that same intent look. He runs his fingers through her hair, tucks it behind her ears.

Alexis suddenly has trouble breathing. She tries to inhale but her chest contracts violently, and she cannot get enough air. She realizes with confusion and embarrassment that she is having a panic attack. She tries to breathe, tries to breathe. Abruptly, she pushes P off of her and rolls over on her side. She gulps in air.

"I'm sorry. I'm sorry. I didn't mean- I'm sorry."

"Whoa, are you ok? What's wrong?"

"I'm sorry. It's a little stuffy in here. I couldn't breathe. I'm going to go get a glass of water."

Simbathe2nd

Dan Shade

Profile: I am 19 years old and have been blogging for about two years. Writing is a strong passion of mine and I am planning to attend college in the fall of 2010, for writing and psychology. My main goal in life is to, not necessarily change people, but to make them think and reason enough to change themselves, like I have in the past few years. Life is a continuous journey of discovery, change, and hope for something better. It may sound silly or childish to some, but I fully intend on changing the world and I hope many join me in my cause along the way.

Wind of Change

Simbathe2nd

I step outside to a gentle wind passing over my face; could it be the winds of change I feel? In the still of the moment everything seems right, but I know it is all a lie. I cannot help but feel the wind is a sign of the world changing, and leaving me behind. It could be that I want to be left behind, for I know the direction this change will take me. I will sit here and allow the wind to pass me by, I refuse to be moved.

Will I ever make a difference in this world, or am I to sit here and allow the wind to hurl the world to darkness? Am I alone in this? I realize with a sorrow that the wind cannot be stopped, even if I stood up against it. Even if a thousand men were to stand in opposition to the wind, it would only pass them by. Wind cannot be stopped from taking its course; all seems lost.

"No" I say, "NO" I scream; I stand up and hold my arms out in rebellion to the wind. Although I cannot stall the wind, the wind will never move me. The wind roars in anger at my challenge to its power. I smile as the wind whips over my face; I stand still. Suddenly a hand grips mine, and another joins his. Suddenly we are a line, standing together. All know it is a lost cause, all care little. Even if the earth would shatter beneath our feet, we would stand here, never to move.

Another wind begins to blow, from where, we know not, greeting that dark wind in a powerful clap of thunder. A storm is brewing in the eastern sky; it is the war to end all war. We stand, hand in hand, as the winds blow and the earth shakes, as the thunder crashes and the lightning strikes; we will never back down; we will never be moved. All the earth is surrounded by darkness; the only thing keeping me, is that hand holding mine. Peace and safety now wash over me as water in a desert; light shines down on me from above, warming my very core. There is no sign of the wind; only silence remains.

Outside Toronto Reference Library

Graham Worthington

Wherever people gather, there those other, half-people are, scarcely noticed, drifting like aimless dust, and every day I see them. If I pause, if I take a casual seat – here, on this low wall – they will settle towards me, shuffling, begging a cigarette, pawing feebly at petty, forgotten desire. They can be found anytime, huddled in shop doorways against the icy wind, or as now, scattered across this broad piazza, blinking in the New Spring sunlight.

They are the residue, the dregs, the ones who could not make it, the dead survivors, the ones we left behind. That man, cheeks black with stubble, not yet forty, shuffling past me the one way as a minute before he shuffled past the other: he moves so stiffly that I thought him crippled with an early arthritis, but now I see that he steps so hesitantly from habit. Long has it been since his stride was warm and quick with purpose.

There, an old man, piled grey hair half crammed into a baseball cap that in his hippy youth billowed jet and glorious black. He blinks, puzzled, at the passing people. Where did his life go to? Who are these busy people whose haste he cannot match and can no longer understand?

Was that how they fell? Was the world was too much, too changing, too busy gathering food to share the banquet, and so they fell, trampled in the stampede of a thousand desires, most of which belonged to others. Did we do this, or was it their own slackness? When the world changed and we leapt to change with it, we nimbly kept our feet whilst they stumbled. We sighed with relief, and quickly kicking the debris aside stood triumphant, erect, and saluted the new day's glory.

And we red, live wires of eager ambition, still glowing hot despite many a cold quenching, we run like crimson threads through the crumbling, grey timber-splinters of the world, We will not yield to dullness, nor too long moan a savage blow. We will have our day, and we will have our day again. We shall not yield.

puella-sapiens216

Marika Turan, born in Australia, but moved to America at the age of five, is presently a college student in Pennsylvania. She is majoring in Accounting and Business, hoping to become a college professor and own a small business. In her spare time she writes poetry and short stories, sells handmade jewellery, and does volunteer work. Some of her other interests include studying Slavic culture, learning Czech and German, travelling, and studying economic development.

Torn Away

Puella-sapiens216

I'm standing outside on the sidewalk under the awning, enjoying my cigarette. Dusk had just settled and so the lazy smoke leaving my fingertips makes a visible dance in front of me. I inhale then exhale slowly, making sure the smoke parting my lips is nice and dreamy. It's cold outside, and I roll up my sleeve to see the time on my watch. 19:26. Damn it, I haven't eaten since breakfast since I was so busy all day with work and getting ready for this date.

We're supposed to meet at 19:30 outside Le Dulce's, then go inside for a nice dinner. We had been chatting online for about four months, and we finally decided on a date to physically meet. I'm nervous as all hell, but standing in the cold with a Marlboro is helping a little bit. I start to mumble through a waltzing cloud of smoke that this may have been a fucking waste of time, when someone taps me on the shoulder.

"Erm, Aleksa?"

I turn around, somewhat startled. The waltz around my head disappears into the dark dusk. Definitely looks as Greek as his picture suggests. I have such a thing for Greeks. He takes my free hand and places a gentle kiss on it, while keeping his gaze on me. As soon as his lips touch my hand I feel my face light up. Holy shit, I haven't gotten a kiss - or any type of romantic contact - in three years. My cheeks must've turned fire red because he also blushed and let out the laugh I could certainly recognise from our nightly phonecalls.

"Oh wow, Peter! I'm so - I'm so - wow! It's so good to finally meet you in person!" I put out my smoke in the snow and hug him. I place a light peck on his cheeks. I hope I don't smell too much of smoke.

We enter the restaurant. The lighting is perfect, the chatter amongst the diners is quiet and low. Someone's playing a violin and walking around slowly - I recognise Vivaldi in an instant.

Dinner goes well. He's just as sweet and kind as I had imagined the past four months. He's going to become a lawyer in several months, volunteers at a nearby hospital, and organises a youth club. He daily visits his ailing brother. He's fluent in Greek and Russian, as well as English. We chat about languages, my time of studying abroad, his current trip to Montreal, music, movies - everything. He shares a funny joke about Elvis, and when it reached the inappropriate ending I burst out in a loud laugh that caught the attention of an elderly couple next to us.

I can't stop smiling, he's so wonderful. I didn't think such a great guy could exist.

"Want to come over to my apartment for awhile? I know you love antique photographs, and I want to show you some. We can even watch a movie." I don't want the night to end, so I quickly say yes to Peter. He pays the bill - $74.86 - and he helps me into my coat and we leave with me resting my head on his shoulder. His embrace is so warm and comforting.

I follow behind him in my car to his apartment, which isn't too far from the restaurant. It's a quaint apartment complex, a hell of a lot better than mine.

I follow Peter inside and to his unit. We enter, and I'm breathless. The entire place was in a smooth, clean black-and-cream contemporary design, with the occasional splash of colour. Spotless.

We sit on the couch and he gives me a glass of wine. Tramin Cerveny - he imported it from Moravia since he knew I loved Moravian wines. We chat for a few minutes, his hand gently resting on my thigh. He catches a glance of the pendant at my throat.

"Is that a locket?" he inquires.

I nod yes, and quickly open it to show him the two small photos inside. Because of how short the chain is, I have to lean into him so he can look at the pictures. I see that his forehead is smooth, but then it quickly becomes distraught.

"Who is this, the man in the right?"

"Oh that's Adam..."

I wear this locket every day. At first I wore it because I missed and loved him dearly, but over time I wore it out of regular habit and never entirely being able to let him go.

I feel the metal of the locket touch my chest again. Peter grabs both my shoulders firmly and looks me straight in the eyes. No more kind smile on his lips. My heart picks up pace.

"Why is *he* still in this locket?"

"I, I, I guess I really never noticed it there. I've worn it every day for three years since he died. Sometimes things become so regular and habitual, you know -"

Slap to my left cheek. I can feel its sting, but it's not so bad since I've got about two glasses of wine in my system. I look at him with my mouth slightly open in shock. His eyes are wild now, and his breathing is heavy. He's had more wine to drink than me - probably about five glasses.

"You're not over him, clearly. Well, I'm going to fix that problem. I love you, and you love me. And that's how it's going to be. I *will* be the *only* one in your life!"

"But, wait –"

He grabs the locket and yanks on it. The thin chain betrays me and snaps. The cold chain falls down into my blouse, and I see the silver locket glisten in Peter's hand. He stands up, grabs a hammer from the kitchen drawer, then smashes the locket on the countertop. I'm still in shock from the slap, so I can't move from the couch. He takes the picture of Adam and walks to the roaring fireplace. The photo floats from his hand and disappears into the red flames.

Peter quickly walks over to me as I'm still shaking in terror at the terrible thing that happened to the only token I had of Adam. He raises his hand, and the last thing I remember is feeling his hand strike my right cheek with a brutal force.

I wake up in my car, and check the time. 9:45. I ache as I gingerly sit up in my driver's seat. I glance at myself in the rear-view mirror. My long hair, which had been in a sleek and elegant bun, was now dishevelled. My lipstick was gone, but I saw a spot of it on my white dry-clean-only scarf. Mascara smeared, and my eyes look like a raccoon. Some blood was congealed in my nose. A purple bruise is on my right cheek. I place my hand at my throat and all I feel is an empty smoothness - I forgot that the necklace broke. A thin purple line marks where the chain had been. I'm bruised all over.

I check my purse, which he must have tossed onto my seat. Everything's still there surprisingly. I light up a Marlboro, and take a deep draw. I exhale slowly, and as I gaze at the dumb and pathetic mess looking back at me in the mirror, I cry.

My poor twin brother Adam – I wish he didn't have to peer down from Heaven and see me like this. I miss him, I need him now.

breaking_expectations
Gloria M

In the simplest terms possible, I am complex. I read,
wrestle and exist."

Scientific Emotion

Breaking_expectations

if what we have is chemistry,
than we need a catalyst.

we have so much potential energy,
but we're going nowhere fast.

you're that equilibrium problem,
that i can never quite figure out.

exothermic,
i want you to keep me warm.

endothermic,
you never give me any of your warmth.

you're complex lab directions,
that leave me struggling to understand.

you're an unlearned concept,
that i want to know all about.

safety is in logic,
i've always been a know-it-all

if knowledge is my emotion,
will you let me know you?

verified-but-still-denied

Chris Lu

Hi, My name's Chris and I'm currently 19 years old. I'm Fujianese, a Chinese regional ethnicity, and very proud of it. I use Xanga as my outlet to talk about issues that I feel should be let out too the public and maybe to vent a little about my life so I can seek some outside opinions. If you follow me, you'll see I'm pretty much a dork and I'll be there for you if you ever need anything. Nice to meet you. :D

So My Bro Came Out of the Closet Today

verified_but_still_denied

Today is gonna be one of my serious, rant mode posts.

My bro just recently came out of the closet...ish. You see, I always kinda knew my brother was gay. Ever since I was thirteen and I cleaned the computer, stumbling across some old files, stupidly clicking on the file that said "juan_and_rico_001", and SH-BLAM. I knew I was straight from the moment I saw that pop up. Then another 50+ files of or so followed. No wonder the computer was so slow...after seeing that stuff... I confronted him about it.

And he told me that he was just confused at first so I believed him... I continued to believe he was straight for the next 3 years. (in that process my gaydar broke)

As I started to "wise up" (finally) I approached him again and he told me that he was bisexual. I was in denial of that because by then I was still cleaning the computer. He was gay. He finally broke from his shell to everyone else in the coming years and became a lot more flamboyant.... everyone knew he was except for..... My parents.

About 30 minutes ago. My brother came out to my mom. And well... Asians will be Asians. My mom said some interesting words in response.

My mom Tearfully: "I'm such a laughing stock. Everything is going down the drain. My mom has cancer, my oldest son needs therapy, and my other son is gay..."

It's interesting to find out again that my mom finds me an embarrassment. What am I saying...?

~~~~~~~~~~~~~~~~~~~~~~~~~~~~~~~~~~~~~~~
~~~~~~~~~~~~~~~~~~~~~~~~~~~~~~~~

So my mom is not accepting that my brother is gay. She is still saying that he is her son...and she's telling herself she should accept it. But she can't. She's not ready to hear this type of information.

Just told my son he should move out to the gay community.... how she's not going to accept it.... She is still in denial. She thinks that being homosexual is a choice. She's telling him that him coming out is going to cause consequences to family, break father's heart, I'll pretend I don't even know you. Thinking that being gay means you're always horny for men. And he's just standing there taking it. I don't know what I am supposed to do or what I should be doing. Someone please tell me what to do.

Kevin's Bad Morning

An excerpt from the Young Adult Novel, *Zorn*

Graham Worthington

Fucking twat, thought Kevin, biting into his pizza savagely. We were supposed to be together, and he fucks off and leaves me.

Kevin had not had a good night. Here a week already, and not a sniff of a girl. Last night he and Michael had sworn not to drink too much, and that way they'd pick up a couple of girls while everyone else were falling down drunk. So he'd taken it steady, but Michael had gone and got pissed up at Ranchers as usual, and then got lucky at Silvers. They nearly couldn't get in, and when they did Mike had got talking to some girl, and slutting about with her all over Silvers, and then they'd both vanished. So where was he this morning? Not in his room, and hadn't shown up by 12 o clock, and so he, Kevin, was sitting at mid-day eating pizza on his own.

He'd banged on the door, but Michael never showed his face, so he never came back last night, unless he'd got so pissed he was still out cold. Did that red-haired slut have a room of her own? If it was her he'd left with, which wasn't certain, 'cause he hadn't seen them leave.

Kevin chewed on his pizza uneasily, and pocked with a finger at the mushrooms, brooding on another possibility. That little slut with the purple eye liner vanished about the same time, that Zorn bitch with the smart mouth who'd been sniffing around Michael a couple of days ago. What if they'd left together? No. Michael hadn't said anything, and in any case he liked things straight, none of these butch girls or fairy boys. So he's been on top of that red-haired piece all night, and was probably on top of her now, and he's said sod you and left me on my tod. Twat. Bitch. Of course I'd do the same, but so what? What'll I do now on my own?

Kevin bit into the pizza and looked across the room glumly. An older guy a table or two away looked up at the same moment, and their glances met. Kevin wagged his slice in vague greeting, then looked moodily out of the window at the passing people. He remembered the dude from Silvers last night, and smelt the scent of a fellow sufferer, for he didn't look too happy either.

Iril didn't remember Kevin at all though. Lump, he thought, some straight dummy stuffing his face. Hit the gym would be a good idea.

The door swung open and a trio of girls came blasting in, noisy and giggling behind dark sunglasses, wet-patched Bermudas pulled hastily on over wet bikini bottoms, bare feet sandy from the beach from where they'd fled in hunger. "Iril," cried their leader, and crashed down into the seat opposite his, hair dripping.

Iril winced at the spray of saltwater drops and spread his hands protectively over his plate. He liked Evren – she was always cheerful – but she couldn't seem to get it through her head he was gay.

Lucky sod, thought Kevin, watching slyly through narrowed eyes while pretending to indifference. That's a nice looking chick, and she's too young for you. More my age. Lay off and send her over here mister. But the chick was all over the dude, standing and leaning over the table, smiling into his face with her big knockers nearly coming out of her top, almost dumping them on his plate. Mangoes! Rub them up against his nose, why don't you, thought Kevin enviously. And the dude was talking to her so easily, not stuck for words.

I wish I could do that, thought Kevin. Now the girl was twisting round the table, half going to the service counter with her feet and half hanging in there with her elbows on the table, still talking to buddy, and now it was her bum wagging at him, Kevin, and she must have made a joke, 'cuz the dude was laughing.

To Kevin it seemed – again – that there was a realer world than his, with realer people in it who were comfortable and knew the rules. Some people were shiny, somehow, and belonged, and people talked to them as if they were important. He felt greasy, and little.

Now the girl was scurrying away to join her friends at the counter, and the dude was looking after her with a funny smile, sort of tolerant, as if she was nothing else but amusing. He must have a bunch of girlfriends, thought Kevin, he doesn't care about her much. He's cool.

As he turned back the man glanced at Kevin, who gave him a smirk of complicity. The guy laughed a little in a self-conscious way, and dropped his attention back to his plate.

No sense hanging out here, thought Kevin, I'll go to the beach and see if Michael's there, the twat.

Kevin walked the promenade from one end to the other, and back again, but there was no sign of Michael. On the way back he saw someone familiar, standing pensive at the water's edge, denim shorts and flowing black hair. Kevin stopped. That Zorn bitch again! But there was no sign of Michael, and the bitch was kicking the sand, sort of lost. Hate you all the same, thought Kevin, yet felt envy at the slim, athletic shape.

Sod it, thought Kevin, might as well go play some games at the RC, Vegan Paintball or Maze World Warrior. I was going to use my credits playing with Mike, but.... sod him. If he's going to piss of like this I'll find somebody else to play them with, and screw him.

So thinking Kevin headed back up Temple Street, almost feeling the warmth of credit ownership radiating from the Status Card in his pocket.

Usually Kevin used up his virtual quota as fast as it arrived, but since he came to Roknor he hadn't played a single VR game, and the credits had pilled up.

There'd been a giganormous world depression years ago

– "it was when you were a rug-rat," Kevin's father sometimes said – and by the time it ended, virtual reality games had been restricted, along with a bunch of other stuff some busybodies thought was messing up the world. A Status Card was needed now to play VR anywhere in European and the U S of A, and it allowed only so much play per month. Some old farts thought this was great, and others raved on about it interfering with personal liberty, but Kevin didn't give a damn either way as long as his allowance appeared on his card, and he could build up his paintball score.

Paintball was ace, 'cuz he was a good shot. The graphics were better on Maze warrior, especially the fancy swords with toothed edges, and the spiked armour, but there was too much jumping about to avoid getting cut. But Vegan Paintball.... Kevin quickened his pace, for already he felt the grip of the gun in his hands, saw the imaginary world of the VR goggles before his eyes. Now if he could only find someone to play against, someone good, but not too good....

Passing the Pizza Palace, Kevin saw the same dude talking to the girls. They were outside now, and the long-haired one was dancing about in front of the guy, twisting on her heels, right up close, water dark hair now drying to a streaked blue.

Lucky sod, thought Kevin, walking around them. I ought to ask him how he does it. Three at once. You'd think two of them would piss off and find somebody else. Perhaps they're in some kind of competition with each other.

The thought made Kevin notice again a poster in a shop window, one he'd read and then stopped noticing as he walked past it a dozen times. "Most Interesting Pic or Story of the Week," and all that sort of crap. They did it every week, and there was a prize. Not a big one, but it would be fun to win something. Kevin plodded on, sweating. He'd beat his score on Paintball today, and sod the beach. It was too hot, and he didn't know anyone here really well except Michael.

Iril headed for the Centre. There was a time when he used to live in such places, but now they bored him. He'd dropped in a couple of days ago though, and seen something more interesting than the range of VR games, namely the tall, blond German guy who ran the section. Not that Iril had learnt his name, but he was older, perhaps twenty-five, and more likely to know his own mind than all these kids. Definitely I'm getting old, Iril thought. Not interested in Virtual anymore, and teenagers are kids to me now. Well why not? Twenty in a few months.

The centre was busy, and so was Hans – I'll call him Hans, thought Iril – and wasn't that always the crap about talking to people where they worked? They had to keep up with their job of course, and you couldn't tell if they were dashing away because they didn't want to talk to you, or if they were just too busy. He could hang about a bit, but it would look really obvious and awkward. When I get there I'll need to grab something fast, or walk out again, or I'll be too obvious.

There's that fat kid again, Iril thought as he walked into the VR section. He looks lost, like he looked in the pizza place. The kid saw him and gave a "hi" sort of look.

Does he play? Iril thought. I don't know anyone else here, so let's go for it. "You play paintball?" Iril could be decisive at need.

"Sure. I'm good at it. And Maze Warrior."

"Come on then, let's play."

And suddenly Kevin had a new friend.

The44thHour

Andrew Weiss

Andrew Weiss is currently majoring in architecture at the University of Houston. Born and raised in Texas, he was homeschooled throughout his minor academic life. His blog contains your recommended daily dose of random and is part of a complete breakfast.

Happiness

The44thHour

Happiness is:

the smell of fall

the sight of friends

the sound of church bells

the welling up of emotion

the long awaited question

the equally timed answer

the greatness of responsibility

the absence of pressure

Loving the love of your L.I.F.E.

Living the life of your Great Love

Happiness is:

short.

Unsatisfied?

See Joy

OhitWontBeForever

Tukha Al-Jibouri

I'm 19, Iraqi, though born and living in Manchester. I'm studying Dentistry, graduating 4 years, hopefully! I enjoy writing; it's one of my main hobbies. Surprisingly, I came to Xanga just to comment a friend's site, but eventually started posting myself. Poetry, short stories, random articles, and now all sorts. I love Xanga, and how it's so tight-knit and supportive of each other, it really is a community, better, a family! I'm really pleased to be part of this amazing project. Xanga's wonderful on the net, but to have it as a material thing is so exciting! Well done to everyone involved! You're all awesome. :D

The Veil

OhitWontBeForever

Let me share with your the lyrics to *The Veil*, by artist Dawud Wharnsby Ali

They say, "Oh poor girl, you're so beautiful, you know? It's a shame that you cover up your beauty so." She just smiles and graciously responds reassuringly, "This beauty that I have is just one simple part of me. This body that I have, no stranger has a right to see. These long clothes, the shawl I wear, ensure my modesty. Faith is more essential than fashion, wouldn't you agree?"

This Hijaab, this mark of piety, is an act of faith, a symbol for all the world to see. A simple cloth to preserve her dignity. So lift the veil from your heart to see the heart of purity.

They tell her, "girl, don't you know, this is the West and you are free? You don't need to be oppressed, ashamed of your femininity." She just shakes her head, and she speaks so assuredly. "See the billboards and the magazines that line the checkout aisles? With their phoney painted faces and their air-brushed smiles? Well, their sheer clothes and low-cut gowns, they are really not for me. You call it freedom, and I call it anarchy."

And this Hijaab, this mark of piety, is an act of faith, a symbol for all the world to see. A simple cloth to preserve her dignity. So lift the veil from your heart, and seek the heart of purity.

They say, "Sister of belief, you are so strong. Your scarf is a flag of this faith where you belong." She just drops her gaze, and then speaks with humility. "I did not wear this shawl at all less than one year ago. I've been judged, misjudged and misunderstood by those who do not know that faith cannot be measured by the garments that we sew. Beauty and faith objects reduced to a fashion show. And this Hijaab, this mark of piety, is an act of faith, a symbol between my God and me."

A simple cloth to preserve her dignity. So lift the veil from your heart, and see the heart of purity. Lift the veil from your heart, and seek the heart of purity. Lift the veil from your heart, and seek the heart of purity...

I was born into Islam, so I didn't technically have to search for this way of life. However, I do believe that there was a point when I "reverted"; when I became no longer a passive Muslim, but an *active* one. I wasn't just praying, I was praying and knowing **why** I did it, I wasn't just fasting, I was knowing **why** I did it, and so on. Islam "injected" itself into my character as well as my actions, words and thoughts. And at that point when I "became" Muslim, I had my own changes, sacrifices and goals to fit my new way of life. This is why I believe everybody's Islam is different. For me, this applies to religion and every aspect of it. That goes for Hijaab, too. So my point is; I'm going to tell you about what Hijaab means to me. And I'm going to do this in the form of a short poem I wrote some time ago about my Hijaab, which I am going to explain line by line.

Hijaab is when your outer beauty becomes your inner beauty; hidden underneath your clothes, not for the eye of the passer-by

So, for me, and I hope for everyone who wears it, the main thing, most obvious thing, is that the Hijaab covers up your apparent beauty, your hair, skin, legs, whatever. That way, it's not for everyone to see, it's not for free, it's a prize, it's wrapped for only those who have the right to see it, those who you *choose* to have the privilege of seeing it.

Hijaab is when your inner beauty becomes your outer beauty; they can see who you are, not **what** *you are, if only they try*

And as for the rest of the people, they will not be able to see you as a "what"; they will only see you as a *"who."* They can't judge you by your hair-colour, your figure, your curves. They will judge you by what you do, what you say, how you behave, because at the end of the day, that's what matters, not how you look. You shouldn't be proud of your looks/figure. *You didn't work for that.* Allah gave you that as it is, so it shouldn't be the way people see you; **pretty** or **ugly**. What you actually worked for and put time into, is your character and your actions. And therefore, that's what people should judge you by, and Hijaab deprives them of any chance of judging you in the wrong way. It's impossible to judge someone on their looks, when you can't really *see* their looks.

***

Hijaab is when your friends become your Deen (faith); when you look at them, you remember Allah (God)

You can't just put a cloth on your head and think you've done it. It is much more than that. In the same way stopping eating is the easiest part of the fast, covering your head, for me, is the easiest part of wearing the Hijaab. With the Hijaab, you don't put it on and stay the same. You put it on and you change. You change the way you dress with it on, you change how you talk, your manners, how you treat people, how you present yourself, and one of the things you change also, are your friends, a lot of the time. The Prophet Muhammad said, ***"Man is influenced by the faith of his friends. Therefore, be careful of whom you associate with."*** If your friends were the type of people to invite you to do bad things, go to bad places, be with bad people, then you've got to lose them. If they weren't, then you can work with each other to change your relationship. You can bring them and yourself closer to your Lord. You can make your friendship an act of worship. You can make your love, of each other, for Him, and you can make your aim to please... *Him.*

Hijaab is when your Deen becomes your friend; it's always in your heart, wherever you are

With the Hijaab, it's a reminder always, wherever you are, whatever you're doing, whoever you're with, that you're a Muslim woman. And that should give you comfort and strength. If you face difficulty for what you're doing for your Lord, you just have to remember that He's on your side. Your faith will get you through; it's your best friend. Allah is your best friend.

*** *

Hijaab is when nothing becomes a wall; everything is deeper than it seems

With the Hijaab, you can show that you have better things to worry about than whether or not every hair is in place. The fact that you don't mind covering your beauty, and you don't feel the need to expose it to all to feel confident in yourself, this shows that you think of bigger things, you have a purpose, and

I've found that it tells people you care; you care about Allah, you care about yourself, and you care about others. You're empathetic, and you're ready to understand others and help.

Hijaab is when a wall becomes nothing; you will always follow your dreams

When I wear the Hijaab, I feel part of something bigger. I'm a piece of a large puzzle. I'm not just one of 6 billion odd people all over the world. I'm connected with so many other girls. Girls I've never spoken to, girls I cannot see. Girls in Africa, Australia, America. Girls everywhere and anywhere. I've never looked at them, but I'm stood with them. That makes me feel stronger, and lets me believe that nothing can stop me following my dreams and being of use in this world today, to be remembered tomorrow. =)

"MISCONCEPTIONS" (read: strange questions) about Hijaab... Answered.

"Do you always wear a pink hat?"
No, no I don't... because (a) it's called a "Hijaab", not a "hat", and (b) I don't wear the same one everyday.

"I thought you wore that same one all the time. I thought you only had one!"
Do you wear the same shirt everyday? *Cough* I have more than one. In fact, I have a drawer-full, and so does my mum. I have all sorts of colours and designs so I can match them with my different outfits.

"So you have special ones that match with your pyjamas, right?"

No. I don't need to wear it in bed. It's only worn in front of men that I can marry. So it is **not** worn in front of my father, my brothers, my father-in-law, my uncles, and grandfathers. It's not worn in front of women, either. And, of course, when I'm sleeping...

"So do you, like, have a water-proof one to wear in the shower?"
No... just, no. (Refer above.)

"Do you wear one in the swimming pool?"

If I am swimming, then I won't be swimming in a mixed pool, because Hijaab isn't only about covering the hair, it's about wearing loose, opaque clothing that doesn't show the skin or figure. So that can't work in a pool. When I go swimming, I go to ladies'-only sessions and I wear normal swimsuits. So there's no need to cover my hair seeing as it's only going to be with other women, and as I explained above, Hijaab isn't to be worn in front of women.

"Did your dad make you wear it?"
Well if he did, I would be taking it off every chance I got when he wasn't around... Do you see me doing that? My Hijaab is my choice. Yes, it's an obligation in Islam, but I am blessed to live in a country where I have the freedom to choose, and if I decided I didn't want to wear it, I would have no human being to answer to. If I didn't wear one, it would be between my Lord and I. So ultimately, it is a choice. And I chose to wear it. And while I'm at it, even though I do believe Hijaab is an obligation in Islam (as some people seem to think all the verses and sayings are not clear enough to prove that), I won't judge the Deen of a girl who doesn't. As the lyrics I posted above say, a Hijaab is between the female servant of Allah and her Master.

"Isn't it weird having to... like, hide from men all the time?"
I don't hide. I pass by men, I smile at men, I speak to men. I just keep a barrier up and I don't act the same around men as I do around women. Yes, *"act"*. Hijaab is not only a veil over the hair. It is a veil over the character. It's a wall you build up to not allow a man to get to know you too well. Your character is your beauty, and your beauty is not for all. And yes, I'm cool with keeping my beauty for a select few.

And a personal favourite:

"Have you ever seen your own hair?"
No, come on. Really, now?

Vignettery

Vanessa E. Lord

Vanessa lives in Wisconsin with her husband and her cat, writing poems, short stories and memory pieces about her childhood in New England.

Bug Spray

Vanessa E. Lord

The hornet buzzed Rose's ear as she bent to empty the dishwasher. She gasped and stood up straight. It flew by her again, and all of the little hairs on her arms went up. Hornets scared her. Always had.

Rose hurried to the pantry and pulled out the big can of FIK (*Flying insect Killer: Good for Bees, Wasps, Hornets... and More!*). She turned and gave the bug two quick shots of FIK and it dropped to the kitchen floor. She gave it a stomp to make sure it was dead. After folding a paper towel in half twice, Rose used it to pick up the winged corpse and toss it into the trash beneath the sink.

The damned things were in the wall, somewhere in the kitchen. The day that three hornets circled her in the kitchen, she asked her husband to call his friend Ernie (the exterminator) to check it out. Chet first laughed, and then threatened to spray the FIK into her eyes.

Two years ago, Chet would have called Ernie over without any suggestion from her. He would have been concerned; he knew how frightened she was by hornets. That was when they were the Happy Family: Chet, the loving husband and proud father; Rose, the affectionate wife and mother; and Lucy. *Lucy.*

Their marriage was just a little rocky when Rose announced that she was finally pregnant. That was when Chet changed: he'd been a good man before, for the most part, but a bit cold; when his daughter arrived, he thawed. Before she could even sit up straight, Lucy had her father wrapped around her pinky.

Rose finished emptying the dishwasher. Everything neatly in its place, she went into the bedroom to change.

Thinking about those days was pointless, she knew, but over the last few weeks, she was finally able to enjoy the memories, let them play in her mind like video tape, without ending with: *That was before Hilary put the poison in the ice cream.*

Her sister made the "special" sundae for her husband, Joe. She used Aunt Daisy's... recipe. Aunt Daisy served "special" ice cream to Uncle Beeb whenever he misbehaved. Joe had been having an affair.

Hilary placed the sundae before her husband at the kitchen table; then, she went upstairs to lay down, complaining of a headache. Lucy came in from the back door, and must have talked her uncle into sharing his ice cream treat.

In public, Chet clung to his wife; the world saw him as a sensitive man, holding his wife up during a tragedy. No one – not their friends, family, or strangers – would guess that at home, he blamed her. He blamed her for having a crazy sister; he blamed her for letting his little girl anywhere near her crazy sister. Lucy was dead; Rose should be in a cell with Hilary, waiting for lethal injection.

It was just a barrage of loud words in the beginning. The words became more vulgar and Chet punctuated many of them with finger pokes. Later, the pokes became slaps. Now, two years later, she endured punches and kicks. She barely left the house anymore, not without her husband. When she left, she'd come back to interrogation; the questions almost always led to more punches and kicks.

Mostly, she shared Chet's opinion. When Joe and Lucy were pronounced dead, when Hilary threw herself at Rose's feet with her confession – it was a mistake; there was only supposed to be enough in the ice cream to make Joe sick, not kill anyone – Rose blamed herself.

She was almost grateful to Chet for punishing her at first. As life went on without Lucy or Joe, as letters poured in from her sister, Rose's thinking changed.

Yes. It was *her* crazy sister. But it was not *her*.

She asked Chet if he wanted to divorce her. She secretly hoped he would say, "Yes," and leave. Or even throw her out into the street. Instead, he broke her nose.

She called her oldest sister, Eleanor, over in Bratwater. *She'll know what to do.* Eleanor came and got her. Two days later, Chet showed up. He apologized. He made promises. Told her that he still loved her. *Please come home. I need you.* He had cried. His words and tears moved Rose. She left with him, even though Eleanor begged her not to.

Chet took her to dinner for the first time in years. They ate. They talked. They laughed. When they came home, he had cleaned the house, top to bottom. She smiled at him. Thanked him. He kissed her, hugged her, and made her feel that he loved her again.

Three days later, the hornets came. She mentioned Ernie. She'd taken the beating that ensued.

She made up her mind that day. She did not care how, but she was going to get out of there. *Things have to change.*

Tonight was the night. Chet was working late. Rose was going up to the prison, to eat with Hilary for the last time. Give her what little forgiveness she had. *It was an accident. Hilary could never do that on purpose, especially to Lucy.*

Afterward, the plan was to get on the next bus to Bratwater. This time, Rose would stay with her sister. Chet's soft words, his apologies and his tears would not work this time.

She inspected her suitcase one last time. Everything was in order. She put Hunny-Bunny, Lucy's stuffed companion on top of her belongings and closed the suitcase.

She is always with me. Chet walked in just as she headed for the front door.

About an hour later, she woke up on the kitchen floor. Only her left eye would open. Chet was on the phone. *Hilary must have called.*

Chet yelled obscenities into the receiver.

She thinks I'm not coming because... oh, God. She started to get up, but did not get far. Her chest tightened. *He's killed me this time.*

Chet slammed the phone down and turned toward his wife quickly. There were more harsh words, more name-calling, but mercifully, no more blows. He was never going to let her leave him.

After a few moments of silence (silent except for their breathing: his, heavy, hers, raspy), he helped her up. He apologized. Begged her forgiveness. He promised to change. Told her he loved her. Cleaned and bandaged her wounds.

She smiled sweetly and told him she understood. She forgave him. Of course, she still loved him. Of course she'd never leave him.

Rose made Chet a meatloaf and mashed potatoes (his favorite meal). She hobbled, kitchen to dining room table and back, over and over, serving him. As he finished his after-dinner cigarette at the table, she brought him a large bowl of peach ice cream. She smiled as he dug in.

Rose went into the kitchen and threw the now-empty can of FIK into the kitchen trash. *Things are going to change.*

Quoth the Interloping and Much-Recycled Raindrop.

Alyxandri

The milky stare.

The blank slate.

The empty room.

The wish for oblivion,

passage of time.

Life and death in a cloudy haze

for a thousand years

of uninterrupted boredom.

saintvi

Melinda has held many jobs and lived many places in her life. Her proudest achievements are being the wife for 30 years to a wonderful man, BookMark61.xanga.com, and mother to a beautiful and talented daughter, joyouswind.xanga.com, and the many years she spent as a Girl Scout leader. She currently works from her home in southwest Michigan, and has been blogging on xanga since December 2005. Her blog has been syndicated on brainfriednetwork.com since January 2009.

HOW XANGA SAVED ME

saintvi

Not long after I started blogging on xanga, my world was shaken by a series of unfortunate events, to steal a phrase. In the space of 15 months, our beloved husky died at the age of 16, our church life began to fall apart and we eventually left, I lost my job and was deserted by most of my "friends" and my father died. I spiraled down into an abyss of grief and depression from which I'm still attempting to claw my way out. During this period of no father, no job, no friends and no annoying dog nosing my hand onto the top of her head to be petted, xanga was one of only two reasons I found for getting out of bed in the morning. In this community of intimate strangers, *people I've never met have told me they love me, people whose real names I don't know have told me they're praying for me, people who are dealing with more and bigger problems than I've ever had to face have offered me words of encouragement.*

Somebody even told me yesterday that I'm not a loser!

Xanga isn't perfect and there are always things that can make it better, but it's been both friend and therapist to me. For a while, it was even church as I watched a service in Illinois through the magic of Xanga TV. If I didn't have xanga at this difficult period in my life, I'd be a complete recluse, venturing out only to buy food and toilet paper a couple of times a month. Through xanga, I've stayed connected to family, friends and the world in general. It didn't save my life or my soul, but ironically, xanga did save that part of me that yearns for human contact.

I'll leave all the suggestions for "saving xanga" to those who understand the intricacies of driving internet traffic to targeted sites. I'm just grateful that the xanga community was there to save me when I was ready to withdraw from the world entirely.

I love you, xanga.

Wayne McCready Gets a Promotion

disillusionisreal

As Wayne McCready stared across the dining table at Constance he thought, *God, she's beautiful.* He soaked in her porcelain skin, ruby lips and blue eyes. She was perfect.

"Well dear," he said, "I've got to head back to work. I guess I'll see you tonight." He stood and kissed the top of her golden head. "Don't forget to dress for dinner." Constance stared ahead as he left.

With a spring in his step and whistling a merry tune, he approached the office building. Today was going to be a great day for Wayne McCready. He was up for a promotion to Clerk II. As excited as he was, he would be sad to leave his cubicle full of memories and the pictures of Constance tacked all over the cloth walls. The promotion meant not only a move up in pay grade, but a move into a brand new cubicle away from the telephone operators. Their voices repeated the same thing over and over, day after day. "Good morning, Cayuga Heights National Credit Union, how my I direct your call?" He heard their nasally mantra in his sleep. It was enough to drive a man crazy. At least then he would be able to hear himself think.

When Wayne walked into his office that morning, his co-workers scattered to the far corners of their cubicles. The first person he spotted was Beatrice. She knew he had seen her. It was too late to run. She lowered her head hoping that he would think she was preoccupied. Wayne approached her, clucking like a puffed-up rooster about how great his and Constance's evening had gone, the dinner, the wine, the romantic snuggling in front of the fire. Beatrice began to feel nauseous.

"That's nice Wayne," Beatrice said, "but I've got a lot on my plate this morning. I'd love to hear all about your night, but duty calls." She turned and briskly walked in the other direction leaving Wayne to stand there scanning the room for his next target. The rest of the office staff busied themselves with paper shuffling and phone answering duties.

Wayne fashioned himself a lady's man. There were those in his office who would reject his idea, telling him if he asked that he was a short, balding, self-important little oaf with bad breath and body odor.

He went to his cubicle and put his hat on his desk. He stared at one of the many pictures of Constance he had tacked to the grey woven cloth walls. There were too many to count, and where most people had pictures of their whole families, pets, friends etc, Wayne had one subject, Constance. Here she was sitting on the porch swing during the summer, dressed in a halter top and shorts, here in the living room in front of the fireplace in the silk robe Wayne had bought for her birthday. In another she was poised at the kitchen table, cigarette in hand, even though neither of them smoked. Wayne thought it would make a great picture for her to look like a 40's movie star. He scanned the walls and as he did his demeanor changed. He relaxed, his blood pressure lowered, he felt contented again. *Screw you Beatrice*, he thought. *You can't hold a candle to my Constance.*

"You know, Wayne," Mr. Breedlove his boss began, "You've done quite well here according to your yearly job performance reviews. How many years has it been?"

"Going on four Mr. Breedlove," Wayne replied. He adjusted his glasses, then his tie. He hated these meetings; they always made him feel like he had something to be nervous about.

"Well, I don't see any reason why I shouldn't recommend you for the Clerk II position," Breedlove said.

"Thank you sir, Constance will be pleased to hear the news as well!" Wayne tried not to gush, but was unsuccessful.

"Speaking of Constance how is the little woman?" asked Breedlove.

"She's as right as rain, sir, and as glorious as a summer breeze."

"You'll have to bring her to the next company picnic, I'd love to meet her in person if she's as lovely as in the pictures you have all over your cubicle."

"I think she'd like that sir, I'll see what I can do. She loves to get all dolled up, women, you know," Wayne chided.

"Well then, that'll be all for today Wayne, and again, congratulations on your promotion." Breedlove stood and offered a fat, manicured hand. Wayne reached out, then remembered to wipe the sweat from his palms.

"Thank you again, sir," he said. He walked back to his cubicle.

He couldn't wait to get home to tell Constance the good news, and as he passed all of the other clerks he began to puff up even more. Beatrice noticed his expression and couldn't help but be jealous. She guessed that he got the promotion. *Actually, I'll be glad to see him go.* She thought to herself. *He's so... creepy.*

Wayne popped his head into Beatrice's cubicle, disrupting her reverie and making her jump at the same time.

"Did you hear? I got the promotion!" he sang.

"Why no, Wayne, I didn't hear, but thanks for the heads-up," she retorted.

"Awww, are we jealous?" he teased.

"Jealous? Of you? Oh my, aren't you clever!" she laughed. It irked him that she wasn't outwardly jealous, but in fact she was. She'd never let him know.

"I think I'll cut out early, be a dear and cover for me?" he mewed.

"Oh sure Wayne, go ahead. Go home to that pretty wife of yours. You'd better keep an eye on that one, don't know what she ever saw in you." Beatrice waved him away. *Yeah, just go. Turd.* She wondered what any woman would see in a man like Wayne. Must be he had some large assets, she giggled under her breath as he strutted off like a peacock.

"Honey! Put on your dancing shoes, we're goin' out tonight!" Wayne announced as he came in the front door. Constance was at the dining table.

"I got a surprise for you, my lovely!" he said. "Guess what I've got, and it isn't in my pocket!" She continued to look at him.

"Alright, if you won't guess, I'll tell you. I got the promotion, and Breedlove says you must come to the next company picnic, isn't that grand!" He bent to give her a kiss.

"Ahh, my sweet, if you don't feel up to going out, we can celebrate here in our usual way." Wayne winked at Constance, knowing she'd catch his meaning.

"I'll just go wash up and meet you on the couch then," he said. He dashed upstairs and quickly returned with her black negligee and high heels.

"Here, I brought you my favorite." he purred, as he led her to the couch. As he began to disrobe, he also took off Constance's clothes. She gazed at him with a pouty, ruby Mona Lisa smile, so secret in its meaning that only he knew what she was thinking.

"Ahhh, finally....are we ready to celebrate, my dear?" Wayne asked as he slowly
spread her legs, his hand gliding up her perfectly formed thigh to her soft round belly and across one perfect 36C breast. He shuddered while he entered her and breathed in her perfume. Grunting, he bucked and thrust, yelling her name as he came, "CONSTAAAAAAANCE!" She never moved an inch. He fell off her, smiling broadly.

Your Bird

Vanessa E. Lord

The coo, the whirr
The flutter of wings
Your bird
Looks up to you
And she still sings.

Marbled, mottled
Cream and gray
Made of stone
But she won't stay
Your bird
Is no one's bird
Not anymore.

I wonder…
Is there a scar
Where her wing,
Once broken
Lifts
Toward the sky?

Not content
To call down to you
From a limb up high
Your bird
Is her own bird
And no one
Owns the sky.

I'm Selling My Ferrari

Lost-In-Reverie

I'm selling my Ferrari.

It was a tough decision, but I have to do it. It's just not good for me anymore. Don't get me wrong, it's not that I don't like it. I love it, and I'm going to miss it like hell. But the joyriding is coming to an end. It was a rash, impulsive, and reckless decision that turned out to be too much fun to give up. Besides, it made me feel good. Scratch that. It made me feel amazing. I mean, come on. When you're driving something like that, it's impossible not to feel confident and sexy, right? Like, if you can get a car like that, you just feel better about yourself all the time. I learned that this feeling is fleeting but damn did it feel great for a while.

Walking away from it is going to be hard though. I loved that car - well, as much as I could anyway. It is just a car, after all. I knew it wasn't going to be around forever, so it's not like I let myself get unbearably attached to it, but I'll be honest, I was pretty darn attached. You invest that much time and energy into something, and it's hard not to. And I did invest time and energy into it - a LOT of time and energy. Because even when I wasn't driving it, I was thinking about it. You have to admit, it's pretty distracting. In the BEST way, but still, distracting.

The funny thing is, I almost got rid of this thing right off the bat. When I first got the Ferrari, it scared the crap out of me. Ironic, right, to have such a beautiful piece of machinery in front of you, and to be scared of it. I was scared of it though, I was scared of driving it - scared of TOUCHING it - because, let's face it, I'm new at this, and not a very good driver. What if I messed it up? What if it crashed? Because obviously, if someone's gonna fuck something like that up, it's going to be me. That's just the way my life tends to work out.

You don't start out with a Ferrari. It's just not a good idea. Because first off, there's really nowhere to go but down. When you start off with something that awesome, where the hell do you go from there? Exactly. You don't. So now I've gotta swallow my pride, take my ego down a few pegs, and settle for a nice little Honda, or a cute Toyota, and know that it's about as good as I can do. And trust me, when you're cruising around in a Ferrari feeling like the world is yours, getting behind the wheel of a Prius is somehow, not as gratifying. Second, totaling a Ferrari sucks a lot worse than totaling your dad's pick-up truck or your mom's station wagon. You didn't just destroy something that was gonna kick the bucket in the near future anyway - you wrecked something truly awesome. And finally, you don't know how to appreciate these things when you are starting out. Why waste it when you're not even going to appreciate it the way you should? You might as well scoff down a whole plate of gourmet food in one bite and chug your wine - it's the same thing.

But the fact that I'm selling it is important. I'm not just giving it away, or throwing it out, I'm getting something out of this transaction. The Ferrari, of course, remains in perfect condition. Even me, with my clumsy ways did not manage to total it. It's beautiful as ever. And doesn't that make it that much harder to part with? I'm the one that got totaled. I got totaled by sitting behind the wheel of that car in utter fear of messing it up. What kind of way is that to drive a car? It's toxic. So I have to admit that I can't handle the situation as it stands. But I won't walk away empty handed. I've gotten plenty of compensation for my troubles. I learned to drive, I got over my fears of actually taking it out of the driveway, and, at the end of the day, I had a Ferrari, even if only for a little while.

Yea, I'd like a Ferrari. Everybody wants a Ferrari, or something like it. But let's face it - we can't all have a Ferrari. Some of us have to settle for the Honda Accord, and the Toyota Prius. Some of us have to cruise around town in a ratty old pick up truck and a broken down station wagon. But you know, people love those cars just the same, and they manage to feel just as great driving them, even if the rest of us laugh or roll our eyes because to us they hardly look pretty, or useful, or worthwhile. But people love those cars anyway. And they can feel just as amazing when they drive them because they don't need that car to legitimate them.

They can do that just fine on their own.

www.elizabethzelvin.com

Elizabeth Zelvin

Elizabeth Zelvin is a New York City psychotherapist, whose mystery series featuring recovering alcoholic Bruce Kohler includes the novels *Death Will Get You Sober* and *Death Will Help You Leave Him* as well as several short stories. She received her second Agatha award nomination for Best Short Story for "Death Will Trim Your Tree." A stand-alone historical story will appear in the August 2010 issue of *Ellery Queen Mystery Magazine*. Liz's blogs on Poe's Deadly Daughters.

Death Will Clean Your Closet

Elizabeth Zelvin

On the Saturday morning when I finally got around to cleaning my apartment, I found a ton of mouse droppings, seven enormous water bugs, and a body. The body lay crumpled like a Raggedy Ann in the back of the walk-in closet. That closet was the jewel in my rent-controlled crown. It made me the envy of all my friends with one-year leases in the overpriced shoeboxes that had replaced most of the old-law tenements and crumbling brownstones on the Upper East Side. The white working-class neighborhood of Yorkville had fallen prey to developers who put in high-rises with Sheetrock walls as thin as a corned beef on rye in a greasy spoon.

She lay sprawled on top of a pile of black plastic garbage bags filled with old clothes that I planned to donate to the thrift shop on the corner and write off on my taxes. Some day. Probably in my next life.

The closet was deep. In the front row hung stuff I actually wore. When I'd brushed my pants and shirts aside with the mop, I'd bumped up against something weirder and more solid than the sexy nighties and assorted female garments left by my ex-wife and a bunch of girlfriends I didn't know any more. I reached for the closet light, a bare bulb on one of those cheap little chains that tend to break off in your hand when you tug on them. This one didn't, but the bulb was dead. And so was she, according to the flashlight.

When you've spent your most sexually active years having alcoholic blackouts, it is literally possible not to recognize someone you've been intimate with. This can happen as soon as the morning after. On the other hand, I hadn't had a drink in 90 days. For three months I'd been clean and sober and celibate except for a fling with my ex-wife, which didn't count, and a one-night stand that had ended badly.

The girl in my closet had a silk tie knotted around her neck. In the dim light, her face looked blue to me. She didn't appear more than mid-20s, with spiky, short dark hair, a row of sparkly ear studs, a little silver star in one pierced nostril, and a rose tattoo on her breast just above the line of her black tank top. She wore faded jeans, cropped above the ankle, with designer holes in them. Her feet were bare. The toenails of the right foot had been painted a glittery silver. It looked as if death had intervened before she got to the left. I had never seen her before in my life.

In AA they keep telling us you can't do it alone. The "it" they mostly mean is staying sober one day at a time. But they also say to practice the principles in all your affairs. The corpse in my closet was my affair, whether I liked it or not. So I called my best friend, Jimmy.

"Bruce. Hey, dude, what's up?"

Caller ID still freaks me out. I'd gotten behind in my technology while keeping up with my drinking. Jimmy, on the other hand, who's a computer genius, is high tech all the way. In the background, I could hear the sounds of battle. I recognized the rebel yell and the hoarse bark of black powder rifles. That made it either the History Channel or Jimmy's interactive Civil War reenactment website. Probably both. Jimmy multitasks.

"I was cleaning my apartment this morning," I began.

"See? I told you that if you got sober, miracles would happen."

"Wait, let me tell this! I burrowed all the way to the back of my closet."

"And did you find Narnia?" Jimmy's girlfriend, Barbara, listens on the extension. She's unbearably perky in the mornings.

"Nope. I found a body. A *dead* body."

The receiver emitted a stunned silence. Then Barbara found her tongue, which never remains lost for long.

"Who is it?"

"I have no idea."

"You're telling me you've been back in that apartment ever since you got out of detox and you never *noticed*?" Barbara screeched. "A *body*?"

"You know it takes a while after detox for all your faculties to come back," I whined.

"Withdrawal is not a synonym for brain dead," Barbara snapped. She's a counselor, and she has no tolerance for alcoholic griping unless she's paid to listen to it.

"Didn't we look in that closet back when we cleaned out the freezer and all that?" Jimmy asked. He'd helped me dispose of some tempting controlled substances.

"The memory is fuzzy, but I think we checked. We didn't burrow."

"There would have been a smell," Jimmy pointed out.

"I did notice a faint stink," I confessed, "but you know my bedroom window looks out on the back of that Italian seafood restaurant on Third Avenue. I didn't think anything of it."

"How long?" Barbara demanded. "When did you first notice the smell? How could someone have gotten in? Where did it come from? Who else has your keys? What about the fire escape? And when? And why?"

"Whoa, there, Torquemada." Becoming a counselor had refined the inquisitorial techniques Barbara was born with. "Let me think."

My brain didn't want to work. I forced it.

"She couldn't have been there that long. She's not stiff, but she's not decaying either." That I would have noticed.

"She?" they both piped up. Guess which of them added, "Anyone we know?"

"No!" I said emphatically. "And yes, I'm sure."

"You'll have to call the police." Jimmy always does the right thing. It comes from his 15 plus years in recovery. Integrity. It's one of the things that always scared the pants off of me about sobriety.

"I can't." For once, I could identify the feeling: panic. I had not enjoyed my prior dealings with the police.

"You've got choices," Barbara offered. It's one of those 12-step slogans that seem so Mickey Mouse until you actually try to live by them.

"Yeah, well, that's no help unless one of them is quietly closing the door and pretending I never found her."

"One day at a time, fella." Another slogan. "One moment at a time." Jimmy has a soothing voice. I began to come back from where part of me hovered on the ceiling looking down and the other part clutched the phone and jibbered. "First things first."

"What *is* first?" Barbara asked.

"How about you start by going back and taking another look at the body," Jimmy suggested. "The police are going to ask a lot of questions."

"Even more than me," Barbara added cheerfully. As she'll inform you, whether you asked or not, self-honesty is one of her character assets.

"You'll stay on the line?"

"We're right here."

I put down the receiver. Jimmy never tires of telling me I need to get rid of my old black AT&T clunker. I do have a cell phone, but I don't have enough recovery to keep it charged reliably.

I marched back to the closet where the door remained open. My clothes hung where I'd left them, pushed to either side. The lighter women's things fluttered slightly in the breeze from the half-open window. The black garbage bags still lay piled haphazardly on the floor. The dust bunnies I hadn't gotten to stirred gently, as if restless. The body was gone.

I stood there with my jaw at half mast. The faint strains of a Puccini aria floated in from the Italian restaurant. The morning cleanup crew and prep chefs were all opera buffs. As if inspired, a blue jay's creaky voice broke into, "Thief! thief!" from the backyard of one of the neighboring brownstones. Somewhere in the building, a door slammed.

I marched back to the phone.

"She's not there any more."

"Hmmm." Living with Barbara, Jimmy's learned to speak a little therapist.

"Bruce," Barbara inquired sweetly, "is it possible that what you've been smelling *is* the garbage from the Italian seafood restaurant?"

"Maybe she was playing possum," Jimmy said. I knew for a fact that Jimmy had never *seen* a possum. He grew up in Yorkville just like me, and neither of us had ventured south of 79th Street until Jimmy's sixteenth birthday. But he loved the Discovery Channel.

"She looked dead to me."

Jimmy had a point, though. A live person hiding in my closet would make a lot less noise sneaking away than someone dragging a body. It still didn't explain what she had been doing in there. Or how she got in. Or who she was.

"How sure are you that you didn't recognize her?"

That one I could answer. "Very."

"Have you slept with any strange women lately?" Barbara is addicted to minding everybody's business, especially Jimmy's and mine. "Inquiring minds want to know," she added, reading my thoughts with ease.

"No!" I didn't have to fake indignation. "Not since detox. Except for the two you know about."

"Before you got sober, then. Did you give anybody a key?"

"I might have," I admitted. I'd been drinking heavily the last month or two before I'd stopped, though I hadn't woken up with anyone I didn't know during that time. But I might have taken one or more to bed. Post-feminist women get up and go home in the middle of the night just like men. If that's what'd happened, I couldn't recall.

"Do you remember your last party?" Jimmy asked. I did recall he'd stopped by for an hour or so. Once the keg arrived, he'd taken off for an AA meeting.

"Only the first two hours, maybe."

A lot of people, not all of whom I knew, had crammed into my apartment that night. It was a couple of days before the Christmas Eve of the final binge and blackout that'd landed me in detox. So anybody might have known the layout. They could have stolen a key. I always lost them, so I tended to keep copies lying around.

"Bruce," said Barbara. "Is your window open?"

"Which one?" I hadn't given up cigarettes, but without the booze to complement them, I no longer took as much pleasure in being half asphyxiated by my own smoke.

"The one leading onto the fire escape."

Duh. That window faced the closet door. I rushed back over there and looked down into the yard. But if she'd gotten out that way, she was long gone.

Relieved as I felt not having to call the police and deal with it, I had lost my desire to clean the closet. I shoved the mop and vacuum cleaner back in there and shut the door without looking. Then I tried to forget the whole thing.

It would have been easier if Barbara hadn't called me at least three times a day with fresh ideas. Could the woman have been retrieving something she'd hidden in the closet? Or stealing something? Had I ever kept dope in there? Did I really think she was dead? What were my mental associations when I saw her? Could she have mummified? Did King Tut cross my mind? My landlord kept the heat way up and loved to pass along the fuel costs to the tenants. So my apartment was dry, but not that dry. Nor was Barbara's well of questions. Was I *sure* I'd never seen this girl? In the neighborhood? At an AA meeting? By the time she finished quizzing me, I could barely remember what I'd actually seen. To the best of my recollection, the girl had looked dead. But in that case, how the hell had she gotten out of the closet? In the meantime, I went about my business. Did enough office temp work to pay the rent. Met Jimmy twice for dinner and an AA meeting. Met my sponsor at a few more meetings. Kept meaning to raise my hand and share, but never did. Took their flak about it. Lied about developing a relationship with my Higher Power. I barely had a relationship with myself. I wasn't used to being asked if I had prayed or meditated today. So I'd grunt and squirm and hope they'd think I meant: well, sort of.

As I walked around the neighborhood, I kept an eye out for the girl with the star in her nose. She couldn't have gotten far without shoes. Maybe she lived nearby.

Instead, I ran into a lot of people I knew. Jacky Doyle, a cop I'd been to kindergarten with. Buddy Russo, the pizza guy, who Jimmy and I had hung out with drinking Colt 45s in Carl Schurz Park over by the East River in our scruffy teens. Cindy Gomez, the first girl I'd ever almost slept with. She chickened out at the last minute. Just as well, or I wouldn't have been able to look her in the face when we collided in the freezer aisle at Gristede's. She was pushing two grubby kids who barely fit in the shopping cart and buying TV dinners. I was blamelessly selecting fish sticks and wondering if it would be any fun to go fishing off Sheepshead Bay in Brooklyn without a six-pack.

Then I met up with a number of people I almost knew, like my next door neighbor, a guy I thought of as Clark Kent. Maybe it was the horn-rimmed glasses. Or that he would have been a lot less nondescript in a red cape and tights. We often found ourselves sticking our keys in the lock at the same moment. Once I ran into him as I tossed a load of household garbage in the dumpster at the construction site a few doors down the street, which you're not supposed to do.

He was doing the same. We nodded and said *Hi*, the way you do. Just a couple of urban outlaws. He was into heavy metal and liked to cook with garlic, and that was all I knew about him. That's New York for you. A city of strangers. Except when it's a village where everybody you grew up with either still hangs at the bar on the corner or turns up in the same church basement saying the Serenity Prayer.

It's kind of like Avalon. Or is it Brigadoon? The old Yorkville occupies the same geographical space as the spiffy new Upper East Side, but they're two separate worlds. In my building, for example, the old ethnic families or their kids have the rent controlled apartments. Old Mrs. Mooney across the hall, whose son Kevin had been killed in Vietnam, would wave and call out, "Feet first!" every time she saw me. She meant that's how they'd have to get her out of her apartment. On the next floor up were the Nagy twins, whose family had come from Hungary in 1956. Jimmy and I had played a memorable game of strip poker with the Nagy girls when we were all 12. Ilona, the one who still lived there, was a lawyer now. Marta was a chiropractor up in Larchmont. She had a house, along with a husband and kids. But I bet she'd move back to Yorkville in a flash if her sister ever wanted to give the place up. Once an apartment got vacated, decontrolled, and renovated, it went over to the other side— the upwardly mobile young who needed roommates in order to pay the high rents.

I looked for the missing woman at meetings too. I saw plenty of girls with spiky dark hair and silver-studded noses. Many recovering women had tattoos. There was a story for every tattoo, many of which I'd already heard. If I stayed sober and kept coming back, I'd probably hear them all. I tried not to look down anybody's cleavage, since thirteenth stepping, or hitting on fellow AAs, is rightly frowned upon. But I did keep an eye out for that little rose.

On the street among the yuppies and the childhood friends, I ran into half a dozen people for whom the three months I'd spent acquiring my sobriety one painful day at a time had passed in a flash, like Rip Van Winkle's 20 years.

"Hey, man, great party!" they said.

I still couldn't figure out how the girl had gotten into the closet. If she'd been in my apartment before, the party remained the most likely occasion. So I asked.

"This may sound dumb—" or "Things got kind of wild that night—"

Whichever way I put it, I felt like a jerk. But I persevered.

"Did you happen to see a girl, not too tall, spiky hair?" My fingers sketched a rooster's comb above my head. "Pierced all along the ear?" I ran my thumb down my own left lobe. "Little silver star right here?" I tapped the side of my nose.

"Hoo hoo," the first one chortled. "Lost your Cinderella? Gotta get that glass slipper out and hit the bars, man, maybe you'll find her there."

"Punk chick, huh," said the second. "Real standout in this part of town—maybe she was reverse slumming up from Alphabet City."

"Nope," said the third, "but I met a real hottie from New Jersey, one a them H towns the other side a the bridge. Practically broke the mattress. Didn't come up for air till Christmas. Hey, that was some party. Ya gonna have another soon?"

Assholes.

Seven days later, one day at a time, another Saturday. Damned if I'd spend this one cleaning. Apart from my reluctance to go anywhere near the closet, the dust had hardly settled yet from last time. I roamed restlessly around the neighborhood. March was almost over, but it wasn't quite spring. Wind nipped at the puny trees just coming into bud along the side streets in the 80s and pounced on crumpled fast food wrappers and flapping sheets of newspaper beside the curbs. I spent more than an hour in Carl Schurz Park just leaning over the railing staring at the East River, where wicked currents eddied between Wards Island to the north and Roosevelt Island stretching down past the 59th Street Bridge.

Late in the afternoon, the wind died and the sun came out. I hadn't slept well the night before. Getting unconscious every night without passing out still presented a challenge. In AA, they say that everything you ever did drunk you have to do sober. So I did something I'd never done sober before. I stretched out on a bench and went to sleep.

I didn't really think I'd doze off. I doubt I slept for more than 20 minutes. But it was long enough for me to dream. I was walking through a thick white mist toward Avalon. Or was it Brigadoon? I knew I had to get there, and I would, if I only went far enough. But the mist went on and on. I thought about giving up. I almost did. Then Jimmy's voice said, "You didn't pass the lamp post." And I woke up.

"You didn't pass the lamp post." What the hell was that about? Where was there a lamp post? Hey, wait a minute. Avalon...Brigadoon...Narnia! You got to Narnia through the back of the wardrobe, which was just Britspeak for a closet. If you didn't pass the lamp post, it meant you hadn't gone far enough.

I leaped up off the bench fast enough to traumatize the nearest pigeons and went tear-assing through the streets toward home. My fingers shook as I stuffed my key into the lock. The hall was empty, but Clark Kent next door had the heavy metal on. I could hear the thumping of the megabass. I finally got the door open, slammed it closed behind me, and double-locked it. Then I made a beeline for the closet.

I pushed impatiently through the first row and the second. In the dark, the clothes on their hangers pressed close around me like trees in the nastier kind of fairy tale forest. Yep, there was a third row. I could make out the dresses and coats from the Forties and Fifties that my mom hadn't bothered to take with her when she'd moved out to

Long Island. They smelled stuffy and old-fashioned. I guess the actual fragrance was mothballs. I even found a few of my father's suits that my mom had never gotten around to giving away or throwing out. I thrust them all aside to left and right.

Beyond all that I finally found a door. I'd had no idea that it existed, though I'd lived in this apartment my whole life. Yorkville old-timers like me had accumulated a lifetime's worth of junk and treasures we hadn't seen in decades and never looked for, because we didn't remember we had them. But Upper East Side yuppies moved into empty spaces.

I groped for a knob or lock. When I found it, the whole thing came off in my hand. I took a startled step back and almost tripped. The screws that had held it rolled around under my feet. When I stepped on them, they fled like mice. From beyond the door, I heard the thump of heavy metal. It was a wild night in Narnia. And I smelled garlic.

An hour later, Jacky Doyle and another cop came knocking on my neighbor's door.

© 2007 Elizabeth Zelvin. This story first appeared in the anthology *Murder New York Style*, L&L Dreamspell.

SheepShot
Johnathan Harrington

I'm Johnathan. I am an 18-year old student, interested in Film Production; mostly focused on direction and screen playing. In my spare time, I usually either watch films, read a book or write. I like to write blogs, articles and short scripts mostly, but I try to delve into poetry and prose every now and then too. I'm also interested in philosophy and religion, which dominate a good part of my bookshelf at home. I also enjoy involving myself in activities where I am surrounded by people, such as theatre and youth politics. Apart from the social aspect of these activities, they require a lot of attention, allowing me to create a personal bond with what I am are working on.

As Venus Herself, by *SheepShot*

People gather round.
The circle is complete, the silence obsolete
"Who'll go first? Tony?"

Rugged and male with scruff
Strong and masculine and buff
he stood up and said, with confidence he lead
"My name is Tony"

Calm

Tony continued
"She was beautiful.
Feisty and fiery, my head left so weary
as she stepped on the meadows that lead to my home.
She drowned my reason,
as she ended the season.

"My heart pulsated, my body elevated
when her hair brushed the grass and the wind lied
It lied," he cried

"It told me her beauty like the heath all across
would wither and end when autumn rolled by
and alone I would lie, alone I would cry.

"It told me her youth would seep in the rocks
and alone she would cry, alone she would die."

Storm

"So I saved her from age," Tony would rage

Calm

And as she lay in my arm motionless, I smiled
I am Tony and I am not a killer.
I am a saviour.
I saved her from becoming old,
And she'll be remembered
as Venus herself."

RaquelHiggins005
Raquel Higginbotham

I'm a student at Kean University and a New Jersey native. I am majoring in English Teacher Education. I am into drawing and art; in fact, I almost went to a completely different school for Animation. I'm very silly, opinionated, and blogging has become one of the biggest parts of my life. I won't quit.

Interruptions in the Night

Raquel Higginbotham

My eyes shot open as I groaned loudly. I gazed sleepily at the ceiling as I slowly turned on my backside. My features settled into a sour frame as I pointed an accusing finger at Him.

"But I don't want to get up" I whined. My eyes began to drift close again when the words 'wake up!' ran through my brain. This mental message didn't scare nor confuse me; my mind bore no questions as I found myself obeying. I hopped down from my loft bed and slipped on my fuzzy pink slippers. 'Why?' I thought as I swung my bedroom door open. A more than familiar message ran through my head saying, "You never know, today could be your last." I grunted as I made my way through the pitch black living room.

I entered the kitchen and peeked over the wall to check if my mother was walking around. Seeing the coast was clear, like a cat, I quickly tip-toed to the computer room. I slowly sat down making sure the chair made no noise; darn chair we really need a new one. I turned the monitor on and eagerly logged on to My Space. "I gotta do what I gotta do right?" I whispered smiling and looking up at the ceiling.

"What is there to say about Grandma?" I began to reflect on the past. Think of the memories Raquel, I thought to myself as I clicked on 'post new blog'. I had never spent much time with the woman so I couldn't say I had a lot to look back on. Can you say writers block? I took another scolding look towards the ceiling, "I know it's not a story!" A thick silence filled the air as my head was still stuck towards the ceiling. Sometimes I don't know if I'm really talking to Him or to myself.

Grandma. Tell me, what can I write about you? I hope your soul hurries up and goes where it needs to go so I can talk to your spirit. All I've got right now is Him and He's not helping much.

"My grandmother died, technically yesterday December 29th, 2006 at 6:15 pm. She was 79 years old. My uncle called my mom from the hospital and told her." I said aloud as I typed. For a moment, I stopped typing and looked up again. 'Why are you making me do this?' I thought as I sighed. In an instant my fingers began to run along the keyboard in a fast pace.

She was sick, I thought. She had to go, it's not like we could've kept her here forever. My fingers quickly lifted from the keyboard. My elbows came down on the desk, my hands cupping my cheeks.

"Diabetes" I said, "She had Diabetes. She also had Cancer, heart disease and only God knows what." My head shot at the ceiling, "What? You should know right?"

My grandmother, Anna B. Wells, wasn't the healthiest of people. Being born and raised in Alabama kept her mind set on a mostly pork diet. She never knew how to cook but that didn't stop her from going down to the closest soul food diner she could find. My thoughts were interrupted as it began to fill with large print.

"What? You know how she died." I said. I was now staring intently at the bright screen as if everything I had to type would magically appear in front of me. "She died of kidney failure." I said aloud as I typed. Yes, kidney failure. It took one week, one excruciatingly long week until the doctors finally rid her of her misery. I remember it like it was yesterday. My head jerked up to the ceiling. "I know it was yesterday! I was being sarcastic!"

I stared at her still form. Her stomach rose evenly with each pump the large machine gave her. Up and down, up and down, my eyes followed each rise and fall. I placed my hand on hers and said, "What do you pray for when you want someone to live, but know they'd be better off dead?" I sighed. Dark brown eyes drifted towards the large door of the hospital. I watched my mom talk to the nurse, her long black pony tail swinging with every head movement. "I wouldn't know what to say to you even if someone told me" I paused. "I guess my departing words have to come from deep within my heart, and all I can think of is good bye."

I smiled at the memory as my fingers began to place themselves on the keyboard. "That's really all I can think of" I looked up again. "Other people's memories? Well I never thought of that." Other people's memories...   ...Well my dad use to tell me some stories about Grandma. If only I could remember. Aha! I've got it, I remember the hospital. The hospital was like her second home, always failing to take her medicine. I guess it's only fitting for her to die in the place she spent most of her time in.

"Yeah, when I first met Anne, I was much younger than I am now" He paused. "Hard to believe right? Your grandmother was a strong woman, she was beautiful too. You have a talent for drawing Raquel, and if anyone asks you just tell 'em you got it from her. She was a singer, something of a harlot in her youth. Let me tell you, when she would take her casual trips to the hospital, she would check herself out the next day and run off to Atlantic City. You know why."

Yeah, I know. How could I forget bingo? My grandmother worshipped bingo like one would the Bible. Gambler, con artist that was her alright. She married about 2 times resulting in fourteen children, 19 grandchildren, and 7 great grandchildren. She would leave the kids to taker care of themselves sometimes while she was out singing at the Key Club or doing whatever the hotshots of the 40's and 50's did. Yeah, not the holiest of women, I know but oddly enough she was always there for them.

I finished typing and logged off of Myspace. "I feel better now" I whispered once again looking towards the ceiling. I must do that a lot don't I? "To an outsider she could be seen as the biggest sinner in the world" I said. I turned off the monitor and sat back in my mothers' office chair. I was always afraid of the dark, but this time the thick shield of black gave me solace as I reflected on my thoughts. I sat longer enjoying the silence until it was almost enjoyable. "Who cares? I loved her just the way she was."

Theacematt2

Matt D

Achieving something of a catharsis within one's work is therapeutic.

Writing is an outlet—one of many.

I'm a full-time college student majoring in Media Production who also works two jobs to maintain my school+life expenses during the semester.

I don't have one identifiable "theme" for my pieces, though they tend to be appreciated by most anybody that stops by my page.

Meeting fellow bloggers is great, by the way.

Tortured Souls

Theacematt2

What was hoped to be an evening planned, rather precisely, had quickly turned into a mere waiting game. Candles, those which once glowed in early anticipation, had long begun their descent, as matched by his hopes. The phone, known often to be lively, remained silent, yet his watch appeared to be screaming; minutes went by. Thoughts, doubts, even time itself seemed to be mocking him, and he imagined her doing just the same.

"Just like all the others," he muttered to himself, "I often wonder what it is I'm hoping to achieve, running a routine like this." His ears and mind grew weary, and that ever-loved self-esteem of his coupled the two for less than enjoyable results. He checked the phone, nobody. Then, the driveway, nothing.

It was beginning to seem as if nothing would ever change. Nights were becoming merely the same, though he didn't exactly know who. . . who was to hold the blame? Yet, plans were made. Yes, plans; made. Plans made by him, for him, him and another. Another? Another... special someone, perhaps? Perhaps not, so it seemed, as this sort of thing had a rather habitual manner of making an appearance.

He then began to wonder, as he often did, how one is to go about finding another. And just who, and what, was he looking for? Another bit of fun? Another empty mind? Or perhaps... perhaps another like himself, though he didn't exactly know who he himself was, either.

His mind went from wondering, to wandering, to searching. Searching the depths of his soul, all in an effort to find... that which was yet unknown. Who was he? And how does one compliment that which is unknown?

It hadn't yet occurred to him, of course, that when one isn't sure what they are looking for, they are more than likely to end up with either nothing, or something wrong. And as for him? He was still rather lost, though he was thinking... which was a start.

That is, until a curious knock was heard upon the door. Such a knock stole the attention of his wandering mind, returned it to it's seated dwelling. While not sure exactly what to expect, he dragged his unwilling body to answer the knocking, and reluctantly opened the door, though merely an inch.

"You came?" he asked.

"Of course... " she responded, "Why wouldn't I?"

"Well, it's just... Oh, I don't know. I've just been doubtful as of late. People seem to be becoming more unreliable with every passing day."

To him it seemed as if her only intent was that of making an appearance, as he watched her stumble into the room and find a seat, wearing an unusually apathetic look upon her face.

Minutes passed; the two of them sat together in a mutual silence, which only allowed more thoughts of misery to attack his senses. His mind became set upon that face, its pursed lips, the eyes dashing about the room; pausing every few moments to dwell on the door, before resuming their aimless search.

He wondered, "What ever could be the matter?" though, not content to leave the notion as a mere thought, he then found the strength to continue making conversation. "Is something wrong?" he inquired, hoping for the chance to ease what appeared to be a mind both troubled and well–spent.

"What could be wrong?" she replied without a second thought. Then, taking a moment to organize her mind, Actually... I mean, no, I'm fine. I'm just... I've... I've had a long day. Work, people, problems; you know?"

"Oh... yes. I—I understand. But—" he motioned to the table across the room, "I've food prepared. And it's good food too," trying his hand at a bit of humor, possibly to brighten her downcast mood, "so long as my cooking hasn't taken a turn for the worse. Come, sit, try to unwind a bit."

She hesitated, before uttering a hushed, "Well... okay," and began to rise.

He watched her with curiosity while she slowly started to edge her way across the room, seemingly unfamiliar with her surroundings. He arose as well, however, his efforts appeared to be in vain; she collapsed to the floor mere moments afterward. Rushing to her side, he noticed a solitary tear beginning its own fall as well. She refused his help, demanding she wasn't to be pitied, that she was, "plenty capable," of regaining her footing, and her belongings, despite the newly broken heel.

"Are you sure nothing's wrong?" he again inquired, receiving only a frustrated sigh in return.

As she began to pick herself up, along most of with her possessions, those of which had become scattered upon the carpet, along with her purse, recently acquired. She remained silent, and after finishing, attempted to make a break for the door. "Woah, woah, woah, now wait just a minute there," he said, barely reaching it before she had managed her escape. "Now. What... is wrong?" he asked, yet again, and stepped away from the door. "I haven't seen you in close to two weeks, and you somehow expect me not to be more than a little curious as to how it is you're acting now? Answer me, if you would. What—in you—has changed?"

"Nothing has changed. Nothing. I just... I can't take doing this any longer."

"Wait, what? What is, "this," in which you're doing, and can no longer take? What do you mean by that?"

"Don't worry a bout it. I'm sorry to have wasted your time. I'll be fine, just... just leave me be," she said, and walked through the now unobstructed doorway.

With that, she was gone.

Garthoon

Graham Worthington

Must all things wait till Garthoon decides to dance?

I saw him first, heavy and proud, his finger raised to forbid

I did not fear him then, nor now, but rather him detested

Heavy and lumbering, he was given the keys

To vast halls, and chambers echoing

Well strewn with subtle toys, and games

Of which he would be steward

And sternly shout, to order all

Full deep his voice, but senseless, empty

Many the troops placed at his hest, and much of iron-
mouthed cannon

With which he slaughtered an army of mice

And we would dance, but here he comes

Dull eyed, he ponders the proposal, fingering the keys

And would have a committee, to turn his back on

And I sigh for the leaping springtime fields

Where ne'er I saw his clumsy tread

Must all things wait till Garthoon decides to dance?

Jonny _Quest

Jon Nelson

Jon Nelson, age 20, was raised on a farm in an unusually liberal family. He previously attended Boston University and will soon attend the University of Kansas where he will study Biochemistry. In his spare time he enjoys reading about politics and social issues. He is an atheist and an ardent supporter of rational thought; in addition, he is unapologetically critical of religion and sacred ideas. He seeks to promote critical thinking and logic through his writing.

Television and the Debasement of Political Discourse

Jonny_quest

Over the past 150 years, America has undergone a monumental shift in our mode of public discourse. In 1859 Americans were still, by and large, a highly literate people, relying on letters and newspapers for the vast majority of their information. The turn of the century saw the advent of the radio, and suddenly the nation became much smaller. News could be broadcasted from coast to coast in a manner of minutes, effectively making the nation a neighborhood. Then, in the 1950s post war boom, the television came to dominate our living rooms. This, I feel, was the beginning of the end for rational public discourse in the USA.

Before our politicians became talking heads on the television screen, people had to rely on discussions with others and their own reading to develop their opinions. Rare would be the citizen that could identify President Polk by daguerreotype, but stating his ideas would readily bring Polk's name to mind. Now we find ourselves in a society dominated by imagery in which just the opposite is the case. These days, if you were to ask a person on the street what President Obama's stance on the Israeli-Palestinian situation is you would most likely be greeted by a blank stare; however, if you were to ask them who their favorite American Idol judge is they would have no problem answering you. It is a lamentable fact that television has transformed us from a culture that once sought out information into one that passively accepts whatever information is spewed forth from the television.

How, then, are we as a people supposed to have an intelligent public discourse if the average person cares only for celebrity gossip or when the new House M.D. will be on? How are we to make an educated decision about our next President, when people know nothing but the few carefully selected soundbites (i.e. Elitist, Maverick, Change, Celebrity, and Lipstick on a Pig) put out by the campaigns. By eliminating the public's capacity for critical thinking, television has created a culture in which the best looking, and perhaps wittiest, candidate is assumed to be the best.

It is obvious, then, that our public discourse needs a fundamental overhaul. We must return to the days when a politician's debating and policy-making skills are the most important factors in his/her campaign. We must abandon our reliance on the television to feed us hand-picked and sanitized information. If America is to return to her former glory the nation must be awakened from its collective slumber.

The Sandwich Artist

Alyxandri

Alexis has spent the last hour in a classroom, looking at a slide show of postmodern art using food. Cupcakes with mustaches, frosting, pink frosting. Artistic food porn. Slide after slide after slide. Alexis doesn't get it. Alexis is getting hungry.

"Feed me," her stomach demands.

Alexis walks to the campus Subway. A line of customers is spilling out of the restaurant's double doors. Alexis recognizes two faces from her last class, two faces without names. The postmodern food porn's other victims.

The line moves quickly. Everyone knows what they want, and everyone is eager to get it. Everyone is eager to move along, move along through the line. No one jokes with the "sandwich artists." No smiles are exchanged. Serious faces, deliberate steps, snappy orders. Yes, the business of ordering a sandwich is very serious, not a time to joke around or exchange pleasantries.

"May I help you?"

Alexis is next in line. Alexis makes eye contact with her sandwich artist. Smiles.

"Six-inch vegetarian on wheat bread, please. With swiss cheese."

Six inches really is enough for anyone. Six inches is the average size for a sandwich. Ordering anything bigger would be cruelly insensitive to all of the other average sandwiches. Wouldn't want to make them feel inadequate. After all, they are the normal size- the size between a Jr. and a Footlong. And there is nothing wrong with being normal, now is there?

"May I help you?" The sandwich artist directs at the man in line after Alexis. She says this in a voice identical to the one she addressed Alexis with. She even has the exact same sarcastic, eager-to-please look on her face.

"A footlong meat-lovers sub." The man mumbles with downcast eyes.

Alexis leaves the restaurant with her sandwich, two cookies, and small drink. She finds a picnic table in the sunlight. It is cold and windy outside.

Alexis sets her food down on the table, using her drink to weigh down her cookie bag. She opens a book and unwraps her sandwich. While leaning forward to take a bite, a strong gust of wind blows the sandwich's paper. Alexis catches it before it flies away. While she is distracted, the wind blows her book shut.

For the next ten minutes, Alexis struggles to simultaneously eat the sandwich and read her book while protecting both from the wind. She notices unsurprisingly that no one sitting at any of the other picnic tables seems to share her difficulties. Oh, to be awkward.

Just when Alexis is starting on her cookies, a squirrel calmly approaches her leg, settles near her feet like any pet dog, and stares determinedly at her.

"You want *food*? Is that what you want?"

The squirrel stares.

Alexis leaves an offering of peanut butter cookie on the ground. The squirrel inches toward it. Encouraged, Alexis throws down another chunk of cookie. The squirrel calmly walks up to it. Sniffs. The squirrel gives Alexis a very human look, clearly saying, "You are giving me *this* shit?" It then catapults itself into a nearby bush.

Apparently, beggars *can* be choosers

Felonious Monk

disillusionisreal

Thelonious Monk looks up

From his newspaper as

He sits in the corner café

A scowl crosses his face

As he recognizes you

From your picture on

Page six. "Ahh, he says,

I believe I have met

A Felonious Monk."

You blush, knowing your

Past enters before you,

Always a step ahead.

"Will I never be

Forgiven for my crime?" you say

To which Thelonious

Replies "Karma my friend

Is a cruel twist of fate.

Papa Rice's

Opening chapter, Wake of the Raven

Graham Worthington

The afternoon was near its end, and the narrow street onto which the bar opened was falling into shadow. Here near the equator the sun rises and sets rapidly, the first dimming of light being swiftly followed by the fall of darkness. When that happened the sun-bleached streets of Paa became black canyons, with the occasional oasis of gentle light falling from the dim interiors of its few tawdry cafes and bars.

Errol had caught the first two of his three fish already, tracking them down easily in the small seaport, but the Englishman had proved elusive. Finally Errol had retreated from the sun to the shaded lair of Papa Rice's bar, and there he sat quietly for some time, watching the hot, weary foot traffic shuffle past. He was confident that this was as good a way as any of finding his third and final passenger, for there was little in Paa to entertain the young unmarried Europeans of that town, and Papa Rice's dingy bar was one of their few watering holes. The Englishman was of that kind who reserve their drinking time till after sun down, but he was winding down what affairs he still had in Paa, so there was no certainty of his schedule. And even if he doesn't come, thought Errol with satisfaction, we're still in the money with tomorrow's flight, well in the money, and he smiled in satisfaction, for the Limey was coming now, strolling down the dirty, rubbish strewn street, weaving his way through the jabbering natives as casually as if he were in London.

"Stuart!"

The calling voice was familiar to Stuart; he had heard it often, usually coming to him over the top of a glass, and he peered from the sun-blasted street, squinting into the shadow to see Errol sitting within the shadowed den, beaming and waving to him over the inevitable drink, and he left the dusty street to join him. The American was a man whose company he soon found wearing, but it would be pleasant to escape the monotonous glare of the dying afternoon sun for a while, and besides that Stuart felt the faint tickle of promise. He eased himself cautiously into a one of the tiny bar's battered chairs, raising a finger to the ancient Malay who ran the place. There was not much need for words with Papa Rice; already he was shuffling to the battered icebox where he kept the beer. Whether they sat at his tables daily, or whether six months passed between their visits, still he knew his customer's habits: beer for the young Englishman who had just signaled to him, and something stronger for the older American: Bourbon, if it could be obtained, but more often some impostor of a rougher but equal strength.

"Where's Isaac?" asked Stuart indifferently, not particularly caring. Isaac was the quieter of the two partners, a thoughtful check to Errol's gustyness. The two usually stuck together like brothers, although Stuart knew Errol be of Italian descent, which Isaac definitely was not. Stuart wondered on occasion how the absent young Jew could have tolerated Errol over the years; still, both were from Brooklyn, and they were both insane Yank pilots, so anything was possible.

"Attending to business, like me. Isaac's looking after the details, while I attend to the grand design. Some are good at one thing, some at something else. Which side of business are you looking after?"

"Both and neither. Not being as fortunate as yourself in having the acquaintance of an excellent partner, I'm both the

General and the dogsbody of all my business, except that now I'm no longer in business, so I stroll the streets of Paa, having the occasional drink with other loafers."

Errol laughed. "And this for another two days until the steamer comes, if it comes, and a bunch more days zigging about the islands till it gets to Singapore. And this is a man with money in his pockets! Limeys!" He leaned back in his chair laughing harshly, the ancient timber creaking in chorus. Stuart began to feel the growth of irritation that Errol usually provoked in him, felt conscious of the predatory bite that lurked even in the man's humour. He had known the two Americans for some years, making their acquaintance bit by bit as their paths crossed his. Sarawak, Singapore or the lesser towns of the crowded Malay archipelago; always the two yanks would sooner or later show up, hauling goods here, there; always busy, often useful, mainly dependable, yet always with that air of being not completely trustworthy. Errol had darkened over the years, the tropical sun ripening the Italian in his blood, and now seemed a creature of the South China Sea, wholly lost and foreign to his distant New York home, his bloodshot eyes peering with savage humour at the dirty streets of a host of petty eastern towns, his once lanky body becoming heavier and grosser as the years accumulated flesh.

"Told you before fly boy, you charge to much. Didn't get too much from winding up the business, so it has to spin out. No immediate prospects in England, so it has to spin out more." The glass arrived at his elbow with a clunk, and Stuart took it up with a leisurely, deliberate lack of concern, looking past Errol at the passing traffic of merchants and beggars. A better price was coming; he felt it, for he smelt the unsold goods sitting heavy on Errol's hands, and like all his race, the American saw himself as a salesman and played out his role consciously, shaking hands quickly on a deal, or grinning and rolling with the punch of rejection.

"Fifty bucks," said Errol briefly. Stuart nearly dropped the glass in shock. He had expected an improvement, but not by so much.

"How come?"

"Take it or leave it pal. Let's just say I'm having a generous day."

"If you're having a generous day I'd better leave it. Probably some plan to get me to Borneo and sell me to the headhunters. They like British heads. Plenty of capacity."

"No. No time to bargain. Tomorrow morning we're for Singapore. Full plane almost; one place left."

"Full? Two days ago you said you had nothing to go there for."

"That was two days ago my friend. You were charting the whole damn plane then, and fuel's not cheap. Now we're full, just one seat left."

Stuart took a long pull at his drink, gazing mildly through the glass at Errol. He too sometimes acted out a role: that of the cool collected Englishman, at home and untouched even in the jabbering tumult of an eastern town. It was an easy mask, an often useful way of dealing with the world, and it worked well on Errol, amusing him as the uptight reserve of the British often does Americans. Nor was it far from the truth, for at twenty-seven Stuart was not yet as lost to his origin as Errol, and remained at his core a calm Englishman, deftly handling the swirl of eastern language and primitive culture whilst remaining separate, at all times conscious that he was an out-flung piece of that damp, cold, superior country that had extended its grip well-nigh over the entire world, then in amiable muddle and uncertainty relaxed that grip, and diminished back to a small island.

"Well?"

"All right." The opportunity was to good to miss. At that price, better than two days heaving about on a boat with coolies, cattle and God knows what else, even if the boat came on schedule, which probably it wouldn't. "What time?"

"Seven. And don't be late. I've a bunch of people that that can't wait to get to Singapore, that's why you're lucky. If you're not there – we're gone!"

"Seven it is. But who else is on the plane, who're your important people who need to get to Singy so badly?"

Errol beamed. Usually he was secretive, but success had put him in an expansive mood. "Not who, what. Boat put in at Panwey, left a bunch of crates for some factory. Machine tools and stuff. Boat left for here, they opened the crates, guess what? - wrong crates. So they wired to Paa, can we pick up the right crates when the boat docks here, fly them to Panwey urgent? Factory can't run without its parts." Errol smiled contentedly, and Stuart guessed that their need had called up a stiff price from Errol. Not an unusual thing to happen out here though; he had bawled and shouted after more than one lost cargo himself. Some coolie had boobed, and now someone else would have to pay out the shekels.

"A muddle," he commented, "but you said Panwey, not Singapore."

"Panwey first, throw the crates out, then straight up again for Singapore, quick, before our Arabs start grumbling."

"Arabs?"

"Yer. We were down at the dock waiting for the steamer, and up comes some fat Arab guy in a hurry with another one dancing behind him; got to get to Singapore now, big hurry, business man, needs to close some deal. I told him we could get him there tomorrow, but we had to go to Panwey first, then we'd turn back south for Singy. And if they didn't like it..." Errol waved his hand in the air dismissively, "so they decided they liked it. That's where Isaac is now. Crates to the plane this evening, fly out early tomorrow. North and West for Panwey, then south to Singy, and we'll be there before dark, and hit the town." He smiled. "Better ending the day in Singapore than Panwey."

All was now clear to Stuart. Errol had already made his profit twice over, and was now trimming it with a few more bucks. "So that leaves you with the grand design part. You came to bar land looking for me to fill the last seat. Very kind of you Errol."

"I am indeed a kind man, but there are others beside you wandering these streets looking to leave this great city. Father Bryne and Roger Dawson, both of who I have successfully seized by the ear."

"Roger the journalist," asked Stuart, "a reddish-haired man?"

"The same. You know him."

"I've met him once or twice, that's all. Didn't know his second name. So that's three of us and the Arabs"

"Four. You, Roger and two from Father Bryne. He's not going anywhere, just arranged a passage for two from the orphanage. A nun, and some kid. You behave, you've got a nun watching you."

"With nothing more than a nun on board I wasn't thinking of doing any miss-behaving."

"We've more than a nun on board. The Arabs have a girl with them, a looker." Errol leered as he spoke, an expression that suited the fleshy coarseness of his face well. "Their secretary. White girl, another Brit. A bit skinny for my taste, but okay for you I guess. I like them stacked; tits like temple gongs, that's the main thing."

Stuart grimaced. "I must remember that expression for future use," he answered. A strand of him relished the vigor of coarseness, but it was entwined closely with another, that set women on a pedestal of respect. He found them strange creatures, but fascinating, from another world almost. One couldn't do without them, or, more correctly, without some of them. Certain ones it was very necessary to do without, as he had learned, to his cost. His eyes had brightened all the same.

"Yeah, and remember there's a nun watching you," Errol reminded him. His tone was jovial, that of the fellow conspirator in the man's world where women were a quarry, but he was watching the younger man with regret, conscious of the void of opportunity between them. Here he was nearly forty, and he drank too much, like Isaac often told him. The face that looked back at him from the mirror got grimmer and flabbier every day, he could see that, and the crazy girls that he had known – so many of them, so anxious to be with the handsome young fly boy – they didn't seem to be around anymore. This Brit though, he still had it all before him. He wasn't tall or bulging with muscle, just average; but he had that slim, wiry, compact kind of body that swung into a cockpit easily, like he, Errol, used to have; the kind of body where it was easy to have a girl swinging on your arm, or two. And tough under that cool, soft manner, and probably clever and educated as well. He had been an officer in Burma, hadn't he, and the Brit officers always kept their titles, even when they went back to being civilians. Probably his family had a pot full of money, and he was going home, and he wasn't dumb, wasting his money away. His short dark hair was all one colour as well, and this especially roused Errol's envy, for he was finding streaks of gray in his own thick mane.

Errol dismissed his thoughts brusquely. He was getting soft thinking this way; they would make a pile on this flight, and that would stop Isaac's whining for a while, always "the plane needs this and the plane needs that." Errol sat up briskly. He wasn't all that old, and he was still a dammed good pilot; even Isaac admitted that. "Papa Rice!" he called, and held up two fingers. Damn it all, he'd buy if the limey weren't going to offer.

Stuart sat awhile and casually tried to pump Errol for the British woman's name, but Errol turned perverse and merely wagged a reproving finger. Probably he doesn't know anyway, thought Stuart, but I'll find out tomorrow, despite him; it'll liven up the flight a bit. He was not intimidated by women, for though he had no illusion of being a Don Juan, yet he knew himself to be presentable, and capable in the kind of conversation that he had found his kind of woman to prefer: intelligent without being heavy, witty without being too smart. If he had been asked to describe his looks he would have laughed a little in embarrassment, and said he had a nose and all the other bits, but they didn't fit too well. This was too modest, for though his features were unremarkable they were neat and regular, with a stubborn mouth contradicting mild brown eyes. Women with a taste for a great show of masculinity overlooked him, and this did not trouble him, for they were rarely his type; but those who looked for a man who was steady, without being boring, they found him a catch, and several regretted that he had already being caught.

Darkness had still not dropped its swift curtain by the time Stuart left, for whilst he found Errol's gusty rogueries amusing, he could only swallow so much of his wind. Besides, he had a few preparations left to complete, though not many, for all that he had built up over the years he had turned into cash some days before, and had been merely killing time, awaiting the uncertain arrival of the steamer that called on its way to Singapore. Now he was leaving a little sooner than expected, and he must make a few last goodbyes before filling his single suitcase and winding the little traveling alarm. Tomorrow would bring the end of Paa and all the other places of the East in which he had worked, the end of the draining tropical heat, the end of the dirty, bustling towns and cities where a dozen languages strove together in tumult, the end of the life he had toiled to make there. He would miss it, but he was glad to go. It was time to move on, time to fly for a colder,

calmer land, even as Jennifer had done.

Convicted

Theacematt2

Pull the curtain, Take a step,
Let the water beat down upon me.

Body standing, Mind racing,
My thoughts, they... I find,
I find clouded my every action.

Raise the water, make it hot,
Rinse what's there, it should be not,
Let me, become clean, this instant.

Silent, the room,
Yet everything, I hear.
Thoughts return,
again shrouding an attempt.

Begin to dwell on the past,
No, forget it, it's the past,
Simply a move, made, without a purpose.

Try to stratch away,
yet still, I can feel it,
this decay, still It stays;
I dislike it.

Quick soap!
Rinse Wipe!
Claw!

These moves.
They're made in vain,
For it remains.
Satisfied, Fed, Content.

This, this should not be,
I'm aware.

Convicted

I actually...
Mistakes have been made,
It was mentioned, just today,
Earlier, ambiguous, vague.

Directed to nobody,
None in particular,
Yet each of us knew,
At least, I knew,
I found, I knew I had to change.

Again I stand, under water,
Refreshing, Hot,
I clean outside, but in? No.
No, dare I say? I've not.

Not yet.

I will make,
With Your help,
I will break.
Break this chain for once,
and for all.

No more, not again,
Wait, Can I, Will I lose?
Possibly, yet I'll try,
I won't fail you, yet again,
At least... it's not what I intend.

I hear them, I've heard You,
Through others, yes I've seen.
Acts, they are possible--indeed.

I've broken, I'm, I'm damaged,
A mere failed attempt, at best,
Yet still, somehow, You love me.

Cut the water, Step outside,
These thoughts, still, they fill my mind,
Yet I hear You, Your plan, mine.

imTHEmeowMIXcat

Toni

I was born in Visalia, CA. I spent many years in a small town nearby at the foothills of the Sierra Nevada Mountains, known as Woodlake. I currently work as a Collections Supervisor in Texas, and also attend the local college part-time with the intention of earning a degree in Nursing. I am happily married to an amazing man named Justin, about whom enough kind things cannot be said to do him justice. We have no children yet, but we do have a little dog, named Sox. When I am not working, I love to read, draw, cook, travel and to learn as much as I can about anything I am able.

Things I Rarely Talk About Anymore

ImThemeowMIXcat

In my last entry I shared some old sketches I had made over the years. They are mostly of my hands and feet. I don't necessarily have a preference for those parts of the body; I drew them because they were readily available in my line of sight. For me, my hands are also a constant source of exasperation. They have been since I was 4, since the car accident that changed everything.

My Mother and I were in a major car accident because she was speeding around a 20 MPH turn going about 80 on our way to the lake, where her Mother, my grandmother was waiting. That's the short story.

The long story is that my Grandma and Grandpa had rented a houseboat to take out on the lake that day. They called my Mom and she rushed out the door with me and into her new Toyota. I was placed into a booster seat made for toddlers with my seat belt fastened over my lap, and Mom didn't have her belt on at all. She told me we had to hurry so we wouldn't be left behind. We stopped at my other Grandma's house (Dad's Mom) while there I chatted excitedly with my Uncles, telling them where we were going, and jumping around impatiently in my tattered old bathing suit (it was my favorite one) while my Uncle made me a paper crane to play with on the ride up to the lake.

I remember asking my Mom about 2 miles before the accident happened if we were going to crash, I had leaned over and looked at her speedometer and saw that it said 80, the turns she was making were sharp and my booster seat was sliding slightly. It made me anxious.

Sure enough, we approached a turn in which the road was full of gravel on the shoulder, the car lost traction, Mom overcorrected and it was over. The Toyota flipped more than once. It all happened so suddenly, and yet I felt like what they said only lasted a few seconds may well have been many minutes long.

Mom lifted up and out of her seat from the force of the impact during the rollovers. She hit the steering wheel first, then she was lifted out of her seat and was smacked against the top of the car's interior, then her back/shoulder slammed into the windshield, shattering it, and she was finally flung like a rag doll between the front and back seats where she lay for a long while, twisted at a horrifying angle and with large pieces of glass sticking out of her back. I was terrified. We finally landed upright, about a foot shy of a ten-foot drop-off into an orchard on my side, I realized that I had watched her nearly the entire time. All I noticed on my side of the car, was how the window cracked when I placed my right hand on it to keep from sliding anywhere while we flipped and I was watching her fly around. It cracked like an ice cube in a warm drink, there were lines running quickly from my fingertips to the edges until the window shattered and my entire arm went out after the glass. It didn't concern me, I returned my attention to my Mom and worried meanwhile my hand was smashed repeatedly between the car and the road. I never saw it happen, didn't feel it either. In fact, the lack of pain was the only reason I wasn't freaking out during or after.

When the car finally settled on the side of the road, (thankfully upright) I asked Mom if she was OK, I whined to her asking why my Sinead O' Connor tape wasn't playing anymore, I asked where my origami crane went to, and while looking for it on the floorboard, (it ended up being in the middle of the street, I shrieked bloody murder until the Paramedics brought it to me so he could ride in the Ambulance too, I kept insisting he couldn't fly himself there, his wings were broken.) I looked down at my feet and noticed rivulets of blood snaking down my legs and dripping onto the floor mat, which was full of broken glass. I didn't understand that the blood was mine until I traced the sticky trail up my leg again. I had come to the premature conclusion that I had broken my legs, since in my 4 year old mind, blood = broken. I kicked my legs around to be sure they were ok, and also to get the broken glass bits out of my sandals. That's when I noticed the source dripping steadily from my right hand...the same hand that was out the window getting smashed repeatedly just moments before. I flipped it over and looked at the damage...it was barely recognizable. My index finger was almost completely destroyed, with the bone almost entirely crushed, my middle finger had a chunk of flesh missing on one side, and the pads of my ring finger and thumb were punctured with fair sized chunks of glass sticking out of all of them. There was deep red blood everywhere, but it didn't hurt at all. The most terrifying part of that day for me apart from being put on a stretcher (sans crane at first) and getting rushed to the hospital, was the sound of my Mother's scream when I finally said "Hey, Mom? Ha-ha, look!"

At this point, I feel as though I have to tell you where my Dad was during all this, because he was around and he found out about our accident in the worst possible way. He was working the night shift and when he got home to our studio apartment and was not greeted enthusiastically by me and noticed Mom wasn't there either, he was confused. He drove to his Mom's house for food and my Uncles told him where we had gone to. He and my Uncle decided to ride up there together to join us, thinking it would have been a pleasant surprise. It was during the drive up the hill that they found our totaled car on the side of the road in the process of getting towed away, they got out and saw the blood everywhere inside the car, one of my sandals, and so much glass. They drove so fast to the hospital they seemed to get there as soon as we did in the Ambulance. Dad was there with Mom when they were pulling the glass out of her back, and they were both crying while they stood by my bedside while the Nurse rinsed the dried blood off of my hand, picked the glass out of it, and wheeled me to another room where the anesthesiologist was waiting to put me out for my surgery. She put a mask over my face and told me to count backwards from 10...I didn't even make it to 8, I fell asleep staring at my Dad's tear-stained face.

My finger never grew again after that, but I was lucky. If my parents hadn't agreed to let a plastic surgeon to work on my hand and pay the incredibly steep bill, I would have lost my finger for sure. My Dr's name was Dr. Michael Stevens; I wish I had had the opportunity to thank him for everything he did for me. My index finger doesn't bend in the middle as the knuckle is gone, it's the same size as my pinky, and the rest of my fingers are riddled with scars from the surgery...but I am still very lucky. It's an injury no one really notices until it's made obvious, like when I played violin and held the bow with my index finger sticking straight out (couldn't bend it) and when I would draw my hands. Sometimes I miss the feeling of having two hands that are "normal" and I often wish I could clench both fists or move them like everyone else...but even with procedures out there now that can fix it, I refuse to even consider it. How weird, right? Ha-ha...I'm not sure why I refuse...but I guess at this point, my imperfect hands are a part of me that I have become kinda proud of. To me, it shows character. It serves the purpose of telling another part of my story.

Debt-Free

Vanessa E. Lord

Two large platters were placed neatly on the white Battenberg lace. She'd had the tablecloth for years and never used it, waiting for the right occasion. Gracefully draped over the folding game table now, it lent atmosphere to her dinner. Three matching napkins, topped with her good silver, sat on top of the three china plates: white with a platinum ring designed to look like lace edging. A Waterford crystal wine glass accompanied each plate. The platters had taken up more room on the table than she would have liked. There was little room for a centerpiece. She settled for white tapers in her best platinum holders.

Hilary sat and awaited her sisters' arrival.

Half an hour later, she called them. First, she called Eleanor, her older sister, who quietly said she was not coming and hung up. Then, she called her baby sister, Rose; she would not even come to the phone.

She walked back to her chair at the table with slumped shoulders, but she did not cry. She did not really think that they would show, but had let a tiny seedling of hope grow when she received Rose's letter the week before.

Oh, well, she thought as she filled her plate with a sampling of everything from the platters. *Not everything can be fixed.*

At half past eleven, The Priest showed up again. He refused her offer of leftover clams casino and took the seat reserved for Eleanor.

He wanted to take her confession. Again.

She told him for the fourth time that week that she was done confessing. God knew, The Priest knew, and everyone else knew the truth. She did what she did, however accidentally (and who really believed that? Sometimes, *she* barely believed it was a mistake...), and it could not be undone.

She and The Priest took their walk together, not the long walk she had expected. They reached their destination in less than five minutes. She was glad. *Let's just get this over with.*

Her in-laws were there, of course, he in his nicest suit, and she in a light blue dress. They took their seats. "I'm sorry," she wanted to say to them one more time, but she did not. She was done apologizing. Besides –

Sorry don't cut it.

She lowered her eyes, but not her head as she made her way to the table. She climbed up onto it, resisting another look at them. She closed her eyes as the straps were buckled into place. She smiled when she felt the first needle prick her skin.

I'll be debt-free, now, won't I?

Shards_of_Beauty

Kendra

Shards_of_beauty first attempted to sing along in church in February 1989, when she was three months old, melding two of her three great passions in life: Jesus Christ and music. The third is words, which is why she writes songs, essays, and everything in between, and why she is pursuing a career that consists of talking all day: teaching elementary school. A graduate of The Master's College in California, she hopes to eventually teach in an international school outside of the United States.

Soon

Shards_of_Beauty

Soon I'll be done with all the required bits
Of questions that have all the answers
And I'll be ready to fly
Away.
Away into the unknown
Where the answers are more questions
And truth is not a box, but an invitation
Free from the ties that bind us together, this world and I,
With its questions that have no reasons
And pains that have a method in their madness
But won't ever tell a soul
Why.
Why is a question that will fade into the darkness
Along with the broken self I leave behind
As I dive into the pool of light at the end of the tunnel
Where questions are not answers anymore.
The light is the answer
Hiding the truth behind glazed window-glass eyes
And shattered hearts.
It waits in the broken shadows
And haunts the queries that have no reply
Because the answer is waiting for me to become a question
myself
And seek.
And seek, leaving behind pat answers that are only
the face of truth, not its core
Digging into the light
Waiting in the hope that haunts the shadows
Until I fly away on the silent wings of the darkness
To live in the light forever

AND NOW YOUR LOCAL NEWS

saintvi

There are big things going on in the world. Iran is angry, China is controlling, North Korea is sabre rattling, a politician is caught cheating, ABC News is digging a new hole for journalistic standards. *yawn* It's like 1979 all over again except it was Elizabeth Taylor's seven husbands instead of Jon and Kate's eight kids that had everyone's knickers twisted back then.

Not to minimize the continuing crises in other parts of the world, but when it comes to the evening news, the real action is in rural America where felonious deeds are fueled by beer, wacky tobacky and habitually fuzzy thinking and provide more entertainment than any reality television program. We've had a real crime wave in my tiny corner of the boondocks. Federal level crime. Counterfeiting. Oooh!

Yep. The mob has made it to the fruit belt. Four stores were raided recently for selling (are you ready for this?) fake Nike sneakers. Arrests were made. Can you imagine going to prison for selling fake shoes? How humiliating. It's like an Arlo Guthrie song. Listen carefully and you can hear the guitar strumming and the slightly nasal voice intoning:

"What are you in for?"

"Faking the swoosh."

And they all moved away from me on the Group W bench.

That's nothing compared to the mortification of those who actually bought the counterfeit athletic shoes from a gas station. In an area where pride is really, really relative and can involve anything from the size of your earwax to the age of your garden tractor, purchasing fake athletic shoes from a gas station will get you laughed right out of Bert's Breakfast Corner.

But wait, that's not all! Counterfeit money has also been circulated locally. No kidding. In a community where people keep their doors unlocked and money sitting on the counter, a fake Susan B. Anthony dollar coin was passed at a garage sale last week. Now that's just embarrassing. Who would go to all the work of counterfeiting coins so they can buy used crap out of somebody's garage? Only somebody fueled by beer, wacky tobacky and fuzzy thinking. Authorities are taking the case very seriously. The perpetrator is reported to have escaped with a *Seals and Crofts* eight-track tape and a Holly Hobbie nightlight. The victim was so traumatized she went to Staples and spent six bucks on a pen that identifies counterfeit bills. Everyone is on their guard.

The biggest crime wave is down the toll road in Toledo, Ohio, where it's now against the law to park in your own driveway. The crime rate sky-rocketed overnight as minions of the Division of Streets, Bridges and Harbor infiltrated sleeping neighborhoods and cited hundreds of miscreants. Residents are now waking up each morning to parking tickets and attorney business cards stuck beneath their windshield wipers. Apparently the city has lost so much money since the state decriminalized marijuana, they've had to criminalize parking on gravel driveways to make up for the lost revenue. A Twitter-based protest is underway. It consists mostly of tweets saying "Toledo sux" and "recall Finkbeiner." That's pretty radical stuff for Ohio. I'm tellin' ya, it's a powder keg down there.

We now return you to the Jon and Kate Plus Eight marathon.

The Picture of Miscommunication.

Alyxandri

She draped herself across his naked body, settling her head comfortably just below his neck. She conformed gently to the slope of his body like a serpent and hid against his skin like a child. His breathing was slow, heavy, concentrated. She listened quietly to the forced steadiness of it; she rose and fell with it. His wide eyes stared blankly up at the dark ceiling, focusing on nothing. His arms were stiff and unnaturally straight. His unbroken tension was a force in the room. Her calm contrasted with his tension, and his tension made her calm more complete. Her calm was her control.

"That was amazing," he said after a moment or two.

She did not say anything. She yawned obscenely and pressed her face more closely against his skin. Her silence was not avoidance. She was not ignoring him or disagreeing with his comment. It was not arrogance on her part. There was just no need to add anything more.

The sound of rain was distant, but easily heard by the two lovers in the quiet of the room. It was cold outside, warm inside. The warmth radiated from their two bodies. The warmth was evidence that they were inside, together. They were not shut out, not alone.

"How many people have you been with?"

"Eight- no. Nine now," she said after a small amount of consideration.

Rain drops. The sounds of inhalation and exhalation. A small trickle of sweat on his forehead slid back into his hair. The young woman closed her eyes, slowly letting the allure of sleep overtake her.

"...and how many people have you made love to?"

Her eyes flicked open with the slight shock of the unexpected question. She hesitated, uncertain of what to say. She could laugh off the question as if it were trivial and unrealistically romantic. She could smile sweetly and tell him that she made love to all of them the best that she knew how and that none had made love to her. But what she unexpectedly heard herself saying was truth, the truth that comes so easily in the aftermath of intimacy.

"One."

"What was his name?" he asked, no longer breathing audibly. His muscles had relaxed some, and he sounded interested.

"Why does it matter?" she laughed.

"I guess it doesn't," he said. They both stared at the ceiling.

In fifteen minutes, she had fallen asleep on the bed beside him. He stared at her for an hour or so, studying her skin and watching her eyes move beneath her eyelids. He cautiously covered her hand with his. She rolled away from him in her sleep so that her back was facing him. Eventually, he fell asleep too.

In the morning, he awoke to the sight of a piece of folded paper on the bed beside of him. A feeling of irrational panic flared up inside of his chest. He picked up the paper.

Giam,

Thanks for a good time! I had to leave for an early class. You were sleeping so soundly. I didn't want to disturb you to say goodbye. So goodbye!

<3 Anna

Giam stared blankly at the note, at the stupid sideways heart she had drawn. Then he forgot content of the note and just stared at her handwriting, at the wide loops and the silly way she dotted her I's. At the pencil smudges from where her hand had lain against the paper.

Was this normal? Is this how it works? Giam felt a little dazed and unsure of himself. *She could have left without leaving anything,* he reasoned. Surely, the note was a good sign. And maybe the heart was her way of showing affection for him, maybe it was her way of signing "love."

Cheering up slightly, Giam resolved to call her later in the day. He took a long shower in which he thought of the way Anna's skin felt in the late hours of the night. While eating a bagel, he considered the even deepness of her voice. And when he stepped out into the sunny morning, he thought about how the sunlight brought out blonde streaks in Anna's beautiful
dark hair.

Onward

Darkoozeripple

A man rose trembling on the shore
Where the sea had newly birthed him
His hands he ran down his wet form
To clean the slime of old creation
And found his lean limbs ready
For joy and death

Before him lay the forest's tangle
Beyond that rose the beckoning hills
On whose crest stood a palace tall
That gleamed beneath the mastering sun
As though it were of diamonds rare
Yet of tomb's shape

How shall I tread, he asked the sky
But sky gave back no answer
Though parrots shrieked amid the trees
If I tread life, will it not bleed
Lying crushed beneath my feet
So I would die

If I stand silent, will I not rot
Here on this burning salty strand
And all my promise so deny
To ignore thus this un-trod sand
And His gift spurn

The waves crashed violent at his back
The thunder rolled above him loud
With nervous start he stepped out
His paces to the dark jungle
Driven to act

With each hard tread he crushed on life
On snail or grass or butterfly
Much as he placed his steps with care
And from his footprints oozed blood
Yet up sprang white roses also

To his relief
And the grim crimson of the one
Added fire to the other's calm
And the cool beauty of the one
Made excuse for the other's gore
In purpose twined

This Girl Walking

Alyxandri

This girl walking in front of me- wow, is she gorgeous. Gorgeous in a conventional, childish way. Short with a small frame- almost certainly in her first year of college. Blonde loosely curled hair arranged over one shoulder, spilling down her back. Tight light-colored jeans and a gray sweatshirt. Her hips sway back and forth mathematically as she slowly ambles down the sidewalk. Slowly she walks, with the air of someone who knows that they are attractive, capable of drawing attention. Attractive, but not necessarily engaging. You want to see how she would look without the jeans and sweatshirt.You want to see her with her clothes off because you know that her skin would be flawless and luminescent. You want to see the graceful curve of her thighs and the small V below her slight tummy. But you can in no way imagine intimacy with her. She would lack passion, be inaccessible. She would be like an erotic statue- something to look at but not touch.

A much older man, grubby, smoking a cigarette. His eyes glued to her swaying behind. I look at him, look at her. He is not aware of my awareness. He doesn't blink, just stares at the smallish girl as she walks past him, walks away. Him in his blue uniform. Him with his lust. The phrase "dirty old man" comes to mind. You imagine this guy taking the girl from behind. It kills the purity of my own lust. To see someone else looking at her and imagining doing who-knows-what to her.

Is my lust really any more pure than this old man's? Because I am educated, attractive, closer in age to her? Because I am poetic in my lust? Does it make a difference, really? No, it doesn't. We are the same. We are both just appreciating an average beauty walking down a sidewalk like any other sidewalk in any other college campus.

Andrew F. O'Hara

www.badgeoflife.com

Andrew O'Hara is a retired California Highway Patrolman, freelance writer and educator who spent many years as a child on a farm in the Sacramento Valley. In his adult years, he returned as a police officer and the enchantment of the area inspired him to write a series of stories about its people and charms. Today, in addition to writing, his efforts are directed towards police suicide prevention through his nonprofit organization, BadgeOfLife.com.

The Swan

Andrew F. O'Hara

What is life? An illusion, a shadow, a story, and the greatest good is little enough: for all life is a dream, and dreams themselves are only dreams.

—*Pedro Calderon de la Barca*

Raymond drained the last of his coffee and waved the waitress away. Sliding out of the booth, he dropped several dollars on the table and went up to the register.

"Was everything fine?"

He smiled and nodded as the girl counted out his change. He wondered whose daughter she might be. She could be the child of an old classmate. Or grandchild, more likely. With a glance around the restaurant, he pocketed the change and hurried out into the summer evening.

Raymond was 72. It had been over fifty years since he'd last seen Orland. Now, only the old water tower was familiar from the freeway. The stores had all changed or been boarded up, the old street lamps were gone and the interstate freeway had confused his sense of direction. In the distance, however, he spotted the familiar buttes that marked the direction of the old farm.

Where the crows sat in the old oak tree.

Where he'd met Julia.

Evening was deepening as he drove out of the restaurant. Ahead, the sun bobbed on the hills and disappeared. Raymond rolled down the window and inhaled the mixture of ryes and lemon grasses as he left the town limits behind.

It was almost dark when he reached the field and parked on the dirt. The vacant farm house was a silhouette in the trees. He ignored it. A moment's search was all that was needed to find a freshly piled haystack a few dozen yards from the road. Stiffly working his way down the embankment, Raymond struck off across the field.

As he approached the haystack, he again drew in that wonderful smell of clover and alfalfa and lavenders blowing across the fields. With night falling quickly, summer stars already cast an eerie neon glow on the open field and, nearby, the old oak tree stood proudly, its branches black against the frosty sky.

"You came."

Julia's voice was unmistakable. She lay quietly against the dry straw, bare feet crossed. "I'm glad," she smiled. Extending a hand to Raymond, she added, "It's been far too long."

Looking down at her, he nodded. "I was afraid," he explained. "Afraid you might not be here."

"I was frightened, too, but we can stop being afraid now, can't we? So come!" She patted the straw next to her, smiling brightly. "Come sit and talk to me."

Raymond sat next to her and stretched back against the hay. They began to talk, quietly at first, sometimes with laughter. Soon, the crickets began to sing and they drifted into silence as the frosty ribbons of the Milky Way edged across the summer sky.

Cursing, young Raymond kicked a stone in his path and it ricocheted off the chicken house. The hens' protests only angered the 14 year-old more. He fired a second rock at them for good measure and stormed down the path, leaving the hens and the small farmhouse behind in the darkness. The drunken screams of his mother and his father's bellows grew more distant as he escaped into the field.

"SON of a bitch!" he growled, whipping the tall grass with his stick. A dairy cow raised her head and watched as he passed. Unafraid of the dark, Raymond headed for the high oak tree in the distance. Kicking and swinging a stick in the grass, he muttered his favorite epithets.

"Fuck!" he spat, and kicked a dry cow pile spinning down the path.

"That's my dad's favorite word."

Raymond froze, startled and angry at the unexpected voice.

"Fuck, I mean."

Raymond saw a slim girl standing in the darkness not twenty feet away, watching him with amusement. The clouds of stars bathed her in a grey light. "It's okay. It's a good word."

Raymond kicked at the dirt. "Yeah," he said, "I guess it is. So what of it?"

Raymond knew the girl. He'd seen her getting on the school bus from the neighboring farm. He'd never spoken to her and they had gone their separate ways in classes at school. She seemed nice enough, he admitted—for a girl.

Her arms were crossed and her summer dress fluttered slightly in the warm night breeze. Her wide smile was framed by pigtails and she asked, "So what are you doing out here in the dark?"

Shaking the blond hair from his eyes, Raymond replied, "None of your business, nosey. Besides, you're a girl and its girls aren't supposed to be out at night."

She giggled. Raymond liked the sound and was unsure what to do next.

"So what are you doing out here?" he persisted.

"Oh, same thing as you, maybe. I don't know. I come out here to look at the stars. And think. Or whatever! Is that what you're doing—looking at stars?"

Raymond looked up into the sky. "What's to look at? It's just a bunch of old stars."

She laughed again, more loudly. "Now I know you're teasing me! I'll bet you're always like that! My name's Julia," she said, suddenly serious.

Caught off guard, Raymond looked at her.

She continued. "Everyone calls me Julie, though, because they say Julia sounds stuffy." She twirled around suddenly, her dress spinning, then stopped and faced him with a smile. Her eyes gleamed impishly and she waited for Raymond to speak.

"I like Julia better," he said, feeling foolish. He felt a need to explain. "I don't know—everyone's called Julie. I never heard of a Julia before." He paused, then finished confidently. "Yeah, I like Julia better."

"Okay!" she blurted. "I never heard anyone say it like you do. I want you to call me Julia, okay?"

"Yeah, okay," Raymond answered, uncertainly. "Oh, and I'm Raymond."

"Raymond!" she grinned. She placed a finger to her mouth, thoughtfully. "They don't call you Ray?"

"Naw, just Raymond. Why? Don't you like it?"

"I *love* 'Raymond!' Besides, if I'm going to be 'Julia,' you should be 'Raymond,' right? Kind of like Romeo and Juliet!"

Raymond watched her as she talked. In the starlight her face was silver. The corners of her mouth were curled in a mischievous smile and her eyes danced even in the dark.

He looked around. "I still can't figure what you're doing out here, though. Shouldn't you be at home?"

"No more than you, silly! And besides, my parents don't worry. They know I like to walk, and besides, this is our field and our house is right back there... OH—LOOK! LOOK!"

Julia jumped and danced with delight as her finger jabbed at the sky. Raymond turned and looked, seeing the glowing trail of a meteor as it faded from sight.

Julia clapped her hands over her mouth, still giggling. Between her fingers she laughed, "You must think I'm nutty! I try to count how many I see at night, but I always get excited and lose count. Do you ever do that?"

"Do what?"

"Lose count! You know what I—you're just teasing me, aren't you?" She looked at him, eyes worried. "I guess I'm being stupid, huh?"

Raymond blurted, "No, no, you're not being stupid at all." Sheepishly, he admitted, "I just can't figure out what you're talking about, that's all."

"Oh, good!" she exclaimed, twirling in place again, pigtails flying. "Come on! I'll show you!" She turned in the dark and leaped headlong into the side of a nearby haystack. Dust and grass flew up in a sparkling cloud as she waved to Raymond.

"Come here, Raymond! Come on! You have to see what I mean!"

Hesitant, Raymond followed more carefully and stretched back next to her.

"Now what?"

"Now I know you're teasing me!" she laughed, covering her mouth again. It was a habit he liked. She let out a long breath and settled her head back into the straw. Raymond looked over. A strange girl, he thought. She was just different. She changed from funny to serious and back again so quickly. He kind of liked that.

They were quiet several moments and then she spoke softly.

"My dad brought me out here a long time ago when we were looking for our dog. It was an evening just like this, and we stopped for a couple of minutes and he told me I had to see the sky. So we plopped down in a haystack just like this one and he started showing me all kinds of things I never saw before."

Julia turned towards him, rising to her elbow. "I hadn't ever noticed the sky before. Not really. Know what I mean?"

"Well, yeah—no." Raymond was confused again. "I'm not sure."

"That's okay," Julia continued. "You're like me. You never really noticed things either." She bolted to her feet and stretched out her arms. Her face was beaming.

"That's why you came here, so I could show you! You just didn't know it! Well, here I am—your humble guide!" Arms spread, she danced in a circle, stopped and curtsied. She was clumsy and almost fell over.

"At your service, sire," she said solemnly.

Raymond broke into a laugh. Their laughter seemed to stir more silver dust from the hay. It swirled and made them cough and laugh even more until they choked and started gasping for breath. Holding her stomach, Julia staggered back to the haystack and collapsed beside the huffing Raymond.

When Julia spoke again, her tone was low and melodious.

"Dad told me the best of all times in the world were at night in the summer. He said when it got dark you could see the whole universe. He said if you got lucky, you might even see God."

She fell silent again. The chirping of crickets in the nearby creek was punctuated by the grunts of the frogs. The aroma of clover and alfalfa and lavender was all around them and strong in the air.

"Dad told me," she continued, "that if you were lonely or had some big problem, you'd always have lots of friends up there, especially in the summer. Dad said all you have to do is start counting your friends and all your problems will go away. Know why?"

"Why?" Raymond asked.

"Because you can't count them all, goofy!" she teased. "I fall asleep every time I try! And then I can't remember my problems, because I'm asleep!"

"Look." Whispering, Julia pointed up into the heavens. She scooted closer to Raymond so he could follow her arm and finger. "Up there's a big cross, kind of like a big letter 'T'…" She traced the pattern several times. Can you see it?" After a moment, Raymond nodded.

"It's my favorite," she said. "It's a swan. See? See how the wings spread out and—and see how the neck goes wayyy out…?"

It took several times until Raymond finally saw the shape of the constellation. Like connecting the dots in a game book, he saw that it really did look like a swan.

They lay in the haystack, still listening to the crickets and the frogs and smelling the lavenders. Each wondered if the other was still counting stars. Raymond breathed easily and became absorbed in the wisps and swirls of the Milky Way and the filmy clouds of stars slowly moving across the sky, and his eyes grew heavy.

"Come back tomorrow!"

Raymond sat up with a start, kicking up the dust, and saw Julia standing on the path, hands on her hips.

"Come back tomorrow night, okay?" She tossed her pigtails and ran into the darkness.

When Raymond walked to the field the next evening, Julia was sitting against the haystack, cross-legged and bony knees exposed. He smiled and sat next to her.

He tapped his stick against the dirt and began scratching meaningless lines.

"Your parents fight a lot, don't they?" she finally asked.

Raymond nodded slightly.

"That's okay. We can hear them sometimes, even at our house." She looked into his clouded face. "But we don't have to talk about that if you don't want to." His silence was her answer. "I understand," she assured. "Besides, we've got our friends up there and we have to count them together and talk about them."

Raymond liked how Julia said "together."

She turned to him and looked at him, a deep and curious look in her eyes. "Would you like to do that with me?" she asked.

Raymond grinned. "Oh, all right, sure," he said. "Why not?"

They began meeting every night in the field.

Winter finally came, and with it came the rain and cold that ended their visits. The creek filled from the storms and the water rushed from ditch to ditch, and the crickets and the frogs grew silent. The huge oak tree full of rustling crows stood guard over their field as the winds and blustering gales made mud of the pastures.

Plastic raincoats and body heat and warm breath painted a fog inside the school bus windows, and Julia and Raymond would swap a smile and even sit quietly together. At school there was little time to talk but the days passed quickly. Raymond would watch as she jumped from the bus in front of her house, plastic coat blowing. If he caught her eye, they would wave at one another.

Summers always returned, and Raymond and Julia would begin meeting again at nightfall. Each summer there were fresh haystacks to lay in and talk and count the millions of stars. Julia pointed out more constellations, drawing their shapes in the air until Raymond remembered them all. As they talked, summer breezes brought back more smells of alfalfa and clover and lavenders and they chattered in the darkness and listened to the chorus of frogs and crickets.

When evening ended she always took a moment to draw the "T" in the sky and they would pause to look at the familiar shape before walking back to their homes.

Some nights, they would lay and talk of families or dreams or worlds they wanted to see, of things they hoped to learn. They shared their secrets and talked for hours and listened or vented their anger. When Julia's dog died of old age, Raymond held her hand in the haystack and stroked her arm as she shook with sobs.

Julia wondered aloud, some nights, if she would ever marry; Raymond talked about his parents' drinking and how impatient he was to grow up. But both realized growing up would mean the end of summer nights together. They decided it was best not to talk about it.

One such night, when Julia was sixteen, she broke their silence by sitting up and turning to Raymond, a serious look on her face. Instead of a girl of thirteen, Raymond suddenly realized she was different. She smelled of soft powders and a tiny bit of perfume. She had taken on a gentleness and warmth Raymond didn't quite understand but realized was nice.

So gradually had she begun to use makeup that he'd missed it completely. Even the pigtails had changed. In their place was hair that slid silkily over her shoulders around a face that had changed from baby-round to a delicate oval. Her lips smiled in a way that made him feel curiously different. Her eyes, however, still had the impish gleam of the child Raymond had first met.

"Raymond?" she asked. She drew her knees tightly to her chest and wrapped her arms around them, staring at her bare feet.

He waited.

"Raymond, I'm scared. What if we grow up and both go somewhere different and we don't see each other again?" She shivered in the summer air and looked over at him.

He avoided the look. "I don't know," he mumbled. "I suppose maybe we could get married. When we're old enough, of course," he added quickly.

Julia thought about it. "But people grow into adults and then they stop liking each other and they do all the things like drinking and fighting and hating each other all the time. Could that happen to us?"

Shaking his head, Raymond scratched his stick in the ground. "I don't know. I don't think it could ever happen to us. I mean, if we were going to hate each other, wouldn't we know it by now?"

Julia was silent a long time. "I could never hate you, Raymond. I love you."

Raymond felt the blood rushing to his face and he stared at the ground. Finally, he looked up and their eyes met. "Yeah," he stammered. "Yeah, me, too."

Julia sprang to her feet and pulled him up. "Let me show you something really special," she said excitedly. She grabbed his hand and, putting her finger together with his, pointed up at the swan.

"See where the swan's head is? That one bright star? See it?"

Raymond strained as he peered into the overhead sky. "Yeah," he said, "I see it."

"Oh, look really, really close. If you squint and look hard, you can actually see that it's two stars really close together, one gold and one blue. Look hard!"

Raymond strained. "I only see one."

"Squint harder! One is gold, and the other is blue. They're beautiful!"

Raymond tried for several moments.

"Close your eyes," she insisted. "Shake your head and try again!"

This time he caught it, a glimmering jewel of gold almost touching the other of blue.

"You saw them, didn't you?" she cried happily. Raymond grinned, nodding.

Julia held onto his hand. "Will you make me a promise? Will you promise me that if anything happens to us, if we have to go somewhere or we don't see each other for any reason, will you promise to meet me there?"

Raymond looked up at the swan.

Julia read his mind. "I thought about it. I decided it was a good place for us to meet. Then I won't have to be scared."

"Yeah," Raymond obliged. "Yeah, okay, I'll meet you there, even if I have to build my own space ship—I promise. Does that make you happy?"

"Yes!" Releasing his hand, Julia spun around gracefully and did a long, slow curtsy. "I thank you, sire."

Raymond and Julia laughed as they had laughed so many summer nights before, and Raymond suddenly felt her hands on his shoulders as she kissed him quickly on the lips.

Startled, he blinked. The kiss was gone and he focused his eyes just in time to see her running up the path towards her house.

"Come back tomorrow night!" she called over her shoulder as she ran.

When Julia died that winter, her father had tried to explain to Raymond how scarlet fever could kill so quickly. All Raymond understood was that Julia was gone. He dreaded the last summer of his boyhood.

When warm weather finally came, he walked alone into the field and went to the haystack. He stretched back facing the sky and found the swan. He looked deeply and found the two stars. They were deep blue and gold and very close together.

The arthritis had crippled his fingers and Raymond struggled to get his glasses off so he could wipe his eyes. Julia leaned over with a tissue in her fingers.

"Here," she whispered, "let me get it." She dabbed at the corner of his eye and dried the tear. Clumsily, he returned the glasses to his nose and smiled at her in the darkness.

In spite of the wrinkles on her face, Julia was beautiful. Her grey hair fell smoothly over her shoulders and her eyes still had the impish gleam of a thirteen year-old. She smiled.

"Besides," she pointed out, "You came back to me."

Slowly, Julia rose to her feet and, unsteadily, spread her arms and turned slowly in a circle.

Fearing she would fall, Raymond started to get up, but she brushed him back with her hand. "Oh, pfoo!" she grinned.

She stopped and curtsied. "But thank you anyway, my good sire!"

They both laughed as they had when they were young, and Raymond watched lovingly as she covered her lips with her fingers. He was only slightly aware of the cancer in his body, and the warmth of Julia's smile erased the pain.

Julia came back and snuggled close to his side. "Look", she murmured, pointing into the sky.

Raymond looked up, and they were quiet as they gazed high into the depths of the universe and found the pair of stars at the head of the swan. He could see them clearly, this time, shimmering gold and blue.

And the frogs spoke again to one another and the crickets played a chorus and the breeze blew clover and alfalfa and lavenders across the field as Raymond died in the glow of the summer night sky.

Roses

ReeserTheShadow

They were twelve long, red roses, the first
he had ever given me or any girl.

Not wanting them to wilt, I dried

them. They hung like corpses

whose blood collects and blackens

as they lie against the earth.

Three years have passed,

and the colour of death caught

in once red petals reminds me

that someday he and I will waste

away and in stead of warmth and kisses

we will share one tomb and one skeletal

embrace. Collected together in a casket dark

with death, my skull will smile

to his, glad we are together always.

Children's Response

Alyxandri

It seems as though children respond to their environment more appropriately than adults do. The more I think about it, the more I am certain that something must happen in adolescence that makes us completely lose our minds. We hit puberty and become irrational animals who are completely at the mercy of internalized emotions and our biological urges to socialize and fuck.

A child feels sad when someone is mean to him, when he has been treated unfairly, when he has been abused. He feels hurt when he scrapes his knee. He feels happy when he is *doing* things- playing tag, going to an amusement park. He feels lonely when he is alone. When a child touches a hot stove, the child jerks back his hand. He learns not to touch it again.

An adult can feel sad and not know why. They can feel wounded and be physically fine. In fact, a physically healthy adult will sometimes feel so depressed and hurt that they will stay in bed all day. They will literally be drained and crippled by an emotion that has no apparent source. Adults feel happy when they make themselves numb, when they are binging on alcohol or taking drugs. This is considered a good time- becoming drunk and desensitized while reality morphs in front of their eyes. And adults feel lonely constantly. They feel loneliness as a presence inside of them- not an emotional reaction. They can feel loneliness while having sex, or even during the more intimate act of holding another person's hand.

And when adult get burned, they do not learn from it. They are driven to do that same thing again and again. They throw themselves back into the fire, knowing that they will be burned. And why do they do it? Why do they allow themselves to be hurt again and again? It is because they cannot help themselves. Humans are animals, robots programmed by natural selection to need social interaction. We need to couple, to feel secure, to have sex. Even after being emotionally wounded by a failed attempt at finding a lifelong mate, an adult human will actively seek out another human, even while knowing that they are just following a biological imperative and will likely be burned again when bonding occurs but the coupling unit fails.

Natural selection really does have a sick sense of humor. It makes even the most introverted of us into needy, dependent, overbearing creatures. All because the animals that mate and couple are the animals that pass on their genetic material.

Not to mention, it is sickeningly funny how we have to glorify and romanticize these biological urges with concepts like "love" and "soulmate" and "marriage." A soulmate is someone who shares an overwhelming physical compatibility with you and probably thinks in a similar way as you. So you convince yourself that his person is "meant for you." A marriage is just our way of dressing up and giving respectability to the agreement of two people to be lifelong mates- not that that always works out.

Love is the most overly romanticized concept of them all. Love is chemistry, a need to take care of another person and be taken care of- protection, the subconscious desire to form a family unit with another person. Love is the umbrella term we give to a combination of a wide variety of different emotions. Ask ten people what love is. They will all give you different answers. Do you know why? Because love doesn't exist. Everyone is so certain of their own definition of love because, since love is not a real thing, not set in stone, it can be whatever they want it to be or whatever their own experience points to.

I am so fucking sick of people telling me what love is.

Bottom line. We grow up. We lose our minds. We are driven insane by our constant need to form relationships. We date. We have sex. Most of us reproduce. Our children are people for the first 9-14 years of their lives. Then they lose their minds and become sex and emotion-driven animals like ourselves. A repeating process of pointlessness.

And it is ridiculous how I know all of this in my mind, but still believe in the romanticized notions that human society has created. How I know something but don't believe it. It doesn't make sense. None of it makes sense. Because I am an irrational adult animal.

Mother Lady Moon

Vignettery

"Ellen?" It was a whisper from the open window in her room. The window was slightly open, and the lavender curtains moved softly with the breeze, softly with the whisper.

The little girl's eyelids were heavy; she could only manage to lift them slightly, just enough to see the moon's light coming in between the lavender cotton panels.

Ellen had been in this bed for a long time. It was prettier and more comfortable than the hospital bed had been; the mattress was thicker and the pillows were puffier. The new mother lady – Ellen couldn't remember her name; she always had a hard time remembering names – had brought in the lavender curtains and softy rubbed a piece of the fabric against Ellen's cheek on her first day there. *See? Soft.*

The new mother lady spent most of the day in the yellow and lavender room with Ellen, helping her to eat ("When you're feeling better, we can have hamburgers for lunch," the new mother lady promised, and it made Ellen's mouth water.), and reading to her from books that she said were now Ellen's. "They're all for you," she said time and time again, slowly waving her arm over the pretty white bookcase that was packed with volumes of all sizes and colours. When she told the new mother lady that she didn't know how to read, the soft-spoken woman smiled and told Ellen, "That's okay. You'll learn… when you feel better. Till then, I'll read them to you." Ellen had smiled at her, even though it hurt. The lady went on to tell Ellen that she would be going to school one day soon, where she would learn all kinds of things, and make lots of friends. Ellen looked forward to it.

"Ellen!" The whisper was friendly, but insistent.

"Yeah?" the little girl croaked. Her voice might never be the same; Ellen had heard the doctor say as much. But the soft-spoken new mother lady told her that she didn't believe the doctor.

Ellen turned her head to better face the window, even though her neck and sides still hurt a lot when she moved.

"Come see me."

She clutched Mrs. B, her stuffed bunny, closer to her. The policeman had given it to her; it was the first toy she'd ever had. The policeman and his friends had saved her from the monsters at the old place; his friends took the monsters away, and he rode with her to the hospital. He stayed with her when she was scared; he gave her Mrs. B to keep her company when he couldn't be there. *Joe. That's his name.* Ellen smiled to herself. *Joe's nice.*

"Ellen? You coming?"

"Can I take Mrs. B, too?" The little girl asked, her voice just above a whisper.

"Of course."

It took her a long time to get up, but Ellen did, hugging her bunny to her the whole time. She shuffled over to the chair nearest the window and sat down slowly, wincing with the pains that seemed to be everywhere. She smiled out at the moon, round and blue over the water.

"There you are," the moon lady whispered. "I missed you, Ellen."

The little girl smiled, even though it hurt. "I missed you, too."

"Everything's gonna be all right now, Ellen. You like the new mother lady?"

Ellen nodded. "Yes, Ma'am!"

"I'm glad."

"Are you okay now, too?" Ellen asked the moon.

"Oh, yes," the moon breathed. "I think I look much better here... don't you?"

Ellen took in the vision of the round blue ball over the ocean – right outside of her new window - once more. "Oh, yes," she sighed. "You look beautiful!"

Blue moonbeams caressed the little girl's face, and Mrs. B's. "So do you, Ellen."

scristian

Scott Christian

Scott Christian is a fledgling writer, who not only dabbles in prose and poetry, but is a published game reviewer. His preference is abstract poetry, or works that are derived of multiple meanings. When he isn't writing, he's running a gaming webshow, reading, or enjoying the company of close friends.

Sip

Scott Christian

I stare into the glassy circle
and shake the contents lightly, slightly
The light from my lamp shines
through the sea of numbness inside
I smile briefly and take a sip
I really don't care

I do it not for comfort nor need
so please don't presume. Resume
my habit of simply indulging
on a nectar of barley and hops
I partake in the final drip
It's just there

My cooling unit is filled with circles;
vessels of my apathy

Why?
Why not?

joyouswind

Krysten Watson

joyouswind, with a B.A. in Music through Grand Valley State University, is finishing a Master of Music in Ethnomusicology at Bowling Green State University. Blogging on Xanga since March 2005, at the urging of a friend, she writes primarily about everyday events, with her own approachable and often humorous perspective. Krysten is thankful to the Xanga community for it's instant support network during college and graduate school. There is always *someone*, whether family, friend, acquaintance, or stranger who is willing to provide encouragement to those in need. She is grateful to be a part of this community.

Headless Fish on a Wall

Krysten Watson

My dad has a freshwater aquarium that has housed tetras, catfish, hermit crabs and snails over the years. One particular year...One particular *morning*, actually, I had a bit of a nasty surprise.

Dads really are gross, sometimes, bless them. On this ill-fated morning Dad found one of his tetras floating belly-up and instead of scooping it up with a fish net like a normal person would have done (myself, with a lot of squealing), he plucked it up by the tail between his fingers, carried it to the bathroom and *flung* it into the toilet.

Gross.

Of course, I was still asleep so I didn't witness this, but Lord Almighty, I know he must have flung that sucker like there's no tomorrow. I don't know if Dad was having a bad morning (I would understand, a dead fish puts a damper on the start of the day) or if he had just finished a bowl of Wheaties, but holy cow.

He flushed the Porcelain Express and went on to work.

I woke up and stumbled, bleary-eyed, to the bathroom. Just as I was reaching for the toilet paper I saw IT and froze. I broke out in a cold sweat and blinked rapidly. *This can't be happening! This can't be happening! Oh, God no, please tell me I'm dreaming!* Hand still hovering over the toilet paper roll, eyes wide and pajama pants around my knees and ankles I felt extraordinarily vulnerable in such a hideously *wrong* situation.

A tetra was stuck to the wall next to the toilet paper roll...headless.

EEEEEEEWWWWWWW!!!!!!!!!

With a shaky hand and stilted breathing I slowly unwound some toilet paper and when my body somehow tore off a bit (because it couldn't have been *me* I was still staring in horror at the dead, headless fish on the wall) the spell broke and I had my pants up, the toilet flushed and was dancing to the sink before I even registered the fact that I wasn't still sitting there, hand hovering in the space between myself and the wall, absolutely dazed.

I washed my hands as fast as I could, glanced up and froze again in horror. Yep, it was still there. I ran.

And then I made a Fatal Error. I told my mother. She told me to get it off the wall. I can't imagine that I have protested anything more in my entire life than I did right then. It took all of her will as a Mother and Dictator of the Daughter to get me to do it. She refused to let it stay there until Dad came home seven or eight hours later - a perfectly reasonable option in my opinion seeing as he was the one who got it there in the first place unless headless fish had suddenly taken to flying around and suctioning themselves to bathroom walls for the pure fun of terrorizing teenage girls first thing in the morning.

I cried, I begged, I refused, and yet somehow I still ended up with a wad of toilet paper half the size of a basketball in my hand, staring down a headless fish. The wad hovered over the fish and retreated. Hovered and retreated. Hovered and finally made contact as I bawled and squealed at the same time.

Fish, wad and all were unceremoniously thrown into the toilet, the lid slammed shut, and flushed with such speed that Superman himself would have been impressed. I washed my hands in scalding hot water and didn't bother sticking around to see if the wad would flush or clog. I didn't care. If it clogged the toilet, it was someone *else's* problem. Not *mine*.

I did not use that bathroom for quite a long time. And I swear to goodness, I can *still* see that damned fish's outline on the wall if I look. Almost, if not a full, decade later, I generally avoid looking at that wall. I will stare straight ahead or anywhere else but there unless I have some mad desire to see if I can still see it, which I can.

disillusionisreal

Jeane Spencer

Jeane Spencer is a 2009 graduate of SUNY Oswego, where she earned her Bachelor's Degree in Creative Writing. In 2008, she won the Mathom Fiction Award for the short story "Suicidal Pumpkins," and an Honorable Mention from The Academy of American Poets for the poem "Felonious Monk." Her work has also been chosen for publication in The Great Lake Review. Ms. Spencer resides in Upstate New York with her partner, Dee, son Shaemus, and assorted fur kids: Xiuchi, Edward, Callie, Phoebe, Pocho, and Giuseppe Guppyfish Silverstein.

Suicidal Pumpkins

disillusionisreal

"Damned dandelions," Elmer said to himself as he jabbed at another with the True-Temper Dandelion Digger, knowing he'd be out here all day if he let it get to him. There were dandelions everywhere. They came from the neighbor's lawn, the one with the suicidal pumpkins. There were fifteen pumpkins cramped into a wooden veggie stand. Six were in a row along the stand's ledge. Below the ledge were seven that had made the jump, lying on the grass. Their lawn was a sea of yellow, acres it seemed, of yellow heads ripening to fluffy seed parachutes. They would take flight at the slightest breeze, float away, lazily drifting down the road to his yard to start a new colony, and he hated them. Hated them.

He thought back to a time before hooks, dandelions and True-Temper Dandelion Diggers, back to life on a farm, a girl, Alice, marriage, and the start of farming his own piece of land; five hundred acres of prime soil. The crop put in, harvested. That first had been a perfect season, except for the yellow pom-poms peppering the front lawn. It began with just a few, sprinkled here and there; he paid them no mind, just mowed them over with the John Deere, or made a bouquet of them for Alice's kitchen. Oh, Alice liked them, would play the butter game with the grandkids, would say "Do you like butter?" to one of them, and rub the dandelion under her chin, turning it yellow with pollen. Funny. Yes, she liked that game. And they taught her to make dandelion crowns to wear on her head. They thought that was funny too, grandma with a dandelion crown. Like a hippy chick.

But Elmer had begun to loathe them through the years; he took pride in his crops, pride in his farm, and greatly prized his bluegrass, and that's where the trouble all started.

Elmer and Alice had been married thirty years when he lost his arm. It happened in a grain auger. Some of the corn stalks had gotten caught in the chute. He tried to dislodge them with more stalks, and when that didn't work he angrily thrust his hand into the chute to try and grab them back out. He didn't have time to register the pain before he was knocked unconscious. When he awoke, he was in the hospital with a stub for an arm.

"Don't you worry now, Elmer," Alice said, "I can get the boys to pick up the slack until you're up and about."

"It's not the slack I'm worried about, Alice." Elmer grumbled from his hospital bed. "The boys can tend the crops just fine; it's the rest of the chores I'm concerned with. The lawn needs mowin' and it's time to fertilize before the next rain; it's just started to come in nice and thick." He knew that if he didn't get that fertilizer down before the next rain, there would be burn spots where the grass had thinned out.

"Don't worry now; I'll have the boys take care of your precious lawn as well. You just lie here and rest." Alice said, she gave him a crooked smile and sighed as she picked up her pocketbook and got ready to leave.

"Everything will be just fine. You'll see, just fine." She turned and left him to beg his commiseration from the night nurses.

Resting was all fine in her book, Elmer thought, she hadn't spent twenty years tending to that lawn. She had her garden out back, helped with the fall harvesting and canning vegetables, but he put in the hard work, long days of seeding, raking and watering the dirt with the finest Kentucky Bluegrass seed he could buy. He wanted a lawn so plush, so thick, that you could set an egg on the tips of its blades and that egg wouldn't settle.

Elmer continued to stab at the infernal dandelions, muttering. After he was fitted for the hook to replace his arm, he learned to use it well. He could use it to jab at the dandelions just as efficiently as using the True-Temper Dandelion Digger, but he'd have to get down on his knees, and they weren't in the best of shape anymore. He looked over at the neighbor's lawn, the sea of yellow, the pumpkins lying on the lawn; they never really kept up on it, and it was he who paid the price.

The Finches moved in about eight years ago, and in all that time had never put so much as a flowerbed on the property. This year somehow, pumpkins made their debut along with the sea of dandelions. They never had a garden; Elmer thought to himself, why all of a sudden is he growing pumpkins?

He saw Finch, come out of his house and decided to approach him on the subject. Maybe they could come to some agreement. He could show Finch how to keep his lawn fed, how to use the fertilizers each season so the grass would grow in plush and vibrant. Maybe they could even share the cost and labor, if he could get him to see his vision; a vast expanse of Kentucky Bluegrass, acre upon acre, so neatly cut and pristine. Not a yellow head to be seen. He smiled serenely.

Elmer started across the lawn, the farm stand caught his eye; he walked toward it, stood looking at the pumpkins, his face contorted. He scowled. Eight years of nothing, and now pumpkins? What the blazes was this happy horseshit? Everything else on their property was run down or broken. There were weeds everywhere, some as high as Elmer himself, and now pumpkins?

Suddenly he snapped. He'd had enough. It came up within him. The rage of all the wasted time digging up dandelions that were just going to come back, another popping up where the last one had been, it seemed like an assembly line of yellow heads. He lifted his arm, the one with the hook, and thrust it down into a pumpkin. The hook did its job. He lifted it high over his head, swung his arm, and the pumpkin went flying up, up and over the farm stand. It landed with a thud, cracking in two, spilling its seeds and orange slimy guts onto the lawn.

Elmer looked at what he had done, and he felt good, so good, he lunged for another, and flung that one up, even farther than the first. It was smaller, it went farther, landing with quiet plop as it cracked and imploded. He smiled, then went for a third, a fourth, and on and on until all twenty-eight pumpkins were lying smashed on the grass. His hook was covered in orange, slimy pumpkin guts; he was sweating from the effort, his coveralls splattered with the fibrous insides of the pumpkins. Seeds covered his boots. Twenty years of fighting an ocean of yellow, had turned into a catharsis of orange colored rage. Any idea he'd had of working together with Finch was gone. It was as if those thoughts had never entered his mind. This was only the first strike. He was not done yet.

Alice stared over the top of her knitting. She had watched this unfold in slow motion. Elmer's obsession with the lawn was near to hysterical, like the feeling you got when a fly landed on your food in a fancy restaurant. There was nothing she could do to help; grass got weeds, and flies liked fancy restaurants. She chuckled over the thought of flies in fancy restaurants. There was no way around either, unless you used something that would kill them.

Finch came running to the farm stand.

"What the hell!" he said. "I spent all summer growing those!"

"Just like you spent all summer growing these dandelions?" Elmer sneered. "You couldn't mow 'em down before they went to seed, could you, just had to let them go to seed. Had to let them invade my lawn. You could have done something, anything!"

"I don't care about your lawn; you're going to pay for every one of them, old man." Finch couldn't stand Elmer, always out there bent over looking at his grass, the guy drove him crazy. It was grass for Christ's sake, grass!

Elmer started to kick the pumpkins around, spreading their slimy, seedy guts and yelling, "You want to see what I go through every day? Cleaning up after your mess?" Swinging his True-Temper Dandelion Digger one way and his slime-covered hook the other, he was a sight. Alice, still watching, started to giggle. He was a bull-headed old man all right, she knew that. Wasn't home from the hospital a week after his accident, and he was right back out there with his lawn. Caressing the plush carpet of verdant green, smiling, a far away look in his eyes.

Finch looked around at the carnage, and tried to salvage two smaller pumpkins that at first seemed to have no cracks in them.

Alice set her knitting aside. She was finding this more amusing than alarming; Elmer had gone off the edge. Like those pumpkins, she thought. He'd get tired, look at what he'd done, and offer an apology. Maybe she could collect what she could of the broken pieces and make a few pies out of them, a peace offering of sorts.

Elmer was undeterred. He was rabid. This would end today, one way or the other. Finch turned and came toward Elmer. He shook his head in disgust, face red from anger and spittle flying out of his mouth. He yelled, "You won't get away with this, get off of my property. I'm calling the police! I mean it old man, this is done. If you want war, you'll get war!"

As Finch started to approach Elmer, he stepped in some of the pumpkin guts. They were slippery; he lost his footing and started to fall backwards (which would have been the better way to go). Wind-milling his arms as he tried to catch his balance, he teetered, then fell forward and met the business end of the True-Temper Dandelion Digger. He was impaled, stabbed in the chest, a deep, mortal wound. He looked at Elmer with a mixed expression of surprise and confusion. Elmer stood there, holding the handle of the tool, not knowing what to do.

Oh my God, look what he's gone and done! Alice said to herself as she jumped out of her rocker and ran towards them.

"You stabbed me!" Finch whispered. He was bleeding profusely, the red mixing in with the orange of the slimy pumpkin guts.

"It was an accident!" Elmer cried. "I didn't mean it. I didn't mean to hurt anyone!"

Finch started to fall to the ground. Elmer looked at the handle of the tool he held with disgust. He let it go as if it burned him. Finch keeled backward like a felled tree. He lay there with the True-Temper Dandelion Digger sticking straight up in the air.

Elmer dropped onto his knees next to where Finch lay. "Go call for help Alice." He was calm now, taking in the scene, remembering the day he lost his arm. He looked into Finch's eyes, which were clouding over and staring straight up into the sky, as though trying to see where the handle of the True-Temper Dandelion Digger pointed.

"I'm so sorry," Elmer said, "I never meant for this to happen, I wanted it to stop. I just wanted it to stop."

Finch took one last gasp of air, and was gone. The ambulance came and went, the police took a report. It was an accident, all a tragic accident.

Elmer never recovered from that day. Fall turned to winter, and he seemed to slowly wither away, like the season's last harvest. Alice tried to get his spirits up, going on about this and that as he sat in his chair staring out the window at the farm stand. He never heard a word she said, only her constant sing-song voice off in the distance.

He passed away in the spring, and as he wished, Alice had him cremated. She knew he didn't want to be buried in the ground. To be food for all those underground creatures. To have the roots of the plants that he once loved so much above grab hold of his bones and lovingly cradle them in their twisting, turning way.

Alice was always sensible, but she remembered Elmer always saying different; that she didn't have any good sense about her. After getting Elmer's ashes from the funeral parlor, she took them out to the backyard of their farm house, and spread them into the wind. She giggled as she watched them float away, lazily drifting down the road, toward a sea of yellow dandelions.

I Hold Two Rings

Alyxandi

I hold two rings,
bands of cheap metal
flaking metallic paint,
tacky junk jewelry.

I hold them cupped
like precious gems.

They slip from my hands,
hands raised in supplication
begging for an exception,
weak human hands.

They fall to the floor.
They are falling as I pick them up.

They are spilling droplets of water,
changing shape as I cradle them
as a mother would cradle
her infant child.

I am not a mother.
I cannot protect.

The future is almost
as dim as the past.
It fades as we stand
with our hands in our pockets.

Our eyes lowered
towards this revolving dirt.

PervyPenguin

Optimist Prime

My name is of no importance, but I live in the not-so-sunny part of California. I hope to one day fulfill by dreams to gun down tentacled zombies when the apocalypse comes. I'm young, act even younger. I draw, I eat, I'm asexual, socially-awkward and that's all there is to it.

I Will Never Understand

PervyPenguin

I'm not going to lie, but I don't understand people in the slightest.

There was a time when I believed I had a concept of how people worked. There were nice people and there were mean people. Of course, this was way back when I was a little kid. Even then, I couldn't quite fit in with the rest, but I still felt like I understood them.

The more I grew, the less I understood them. To this very day, I'm turning 20 this year and I still don't understand other people.

All these numbers were thrown into the equation and now, I'm completely lost. I wanted to fit in more than anything when I was younger. However, I never had a single friend, only acquaintances. I tried, really I did, but I could never quite get close to others. I was even put to therapy when I was in the first grade. There's not much I really remember, but I just remember this lady would ask me questions and watch me play. I recall thinking how uncomfortable I felt. I rarely played, I was more of the sit-still-and-day-dream type.

As I was finishing elementary school, people asked if I liked anyone yet. My response was always the same: "I'm not into boys yet."

That excuse will only take you so far. I even faked crushes just to feel some semblance of normalcy. I even faked it in middle school, on this guy who I did feel close to, but for a strange reason. I felt he was different from the other guys I hung out with. I later found out that that was my gaydar going off. No wonder I got along with him so well, right?

Regardless, I felt we were similar because we never really had an interest in dating. The reason I faked a crush with him was because I started hanging out with these girls who said, "Like, oh my god, just admit you like him already!"

I didn't, but I admit it anyway. Because I don't have a linear thinking pattern, this was eighth grade. In seventh grade, I became more "butchy", I would say. I arm-wrestled, I played sports with the guys which was completely different than sixth grade, when I used to ace every subject. I traded brains for brawn. I couldn't fit in with anyone if I was smart. Sure, people talked to me, but that was only to get answers from last night's homework. I changed every year. I was a damn chameleon. I believed that seventh grade was my best year. I was strong, I was confident and I didn't have to worry about   betrayal...yet. Would you believe I made good acquaintances with someone after we fought? Men work in strange ways, but I don't mind it. His name was Luis, we fought, crashed into trash cans and when the teacher came to stop us, we pretended we were friends. The next thing you know, we're walking around the track listening to his KISS album through the same headphone.

That was when Jessie, this annoying dude, just shouted, "Karina and Luis, sitting in a tree! K-I-S-S-I-N-" "*I don't swing that way*!" I found myself yelling that, no idea why, but I did. Whatever, it shut them up, right?

The same happened with this other boy, Michael. I used to play basketball with him and this girl started sticking her nose in my platonic business and said, "You two should just admit you like each other!"

Yeah, because if you play basketball with someone, that means I *totally* want their nuts. She had to have me prove I didn't like him, so I did...

I didn't have to hit him, but I felt that I did. Mostly because she was watching me and I wanted to prove to her that he was nothing more than a guy I play basketball with. Like her
 opinion *really* mattered. He didn't talk to me after that.

Anyway, fast forward to the eight grade, again. I used that "I'm not into boys yet" line a few more times and it didn't work. I didn't get it, how can you tell if you like someone? What do you feel? How am I supposed to feel?

After the this fake fiasco. Some guy took an interest in me, he was from my martial arts class. To be honest, I was suspicious of him. He wore trench coats, he drank, he did every drug grown on the planet. Yeah, I didn't like him. My brother thought he was a good friend though and he constantly brought him over to our house. Ugh. He made moves on me and I didn't like them and stupid me thought, "Maybe I can grow to like him. Maybe, because he likes me, I could finally understand what relationships are about."

He disgusted me and I felt disgusted at myself. He *touched* me and I hated it, but I felt that if I kept letting him do it, that maybe I would like it. After all, almost everyone I knew had sex already, maybe I would like it? I realized this shit was getting nowhere, I only felt gross. So, I broke it off and I felt a weight of my shoulders. Sure, he threatened to kill me in my sleep, but I felt relieved nonetheless. Thank goodness it never gone as far as he wanted it to go. That's the only relief I get out of that. I still regret starting that relationshit in the first place and I still cringe when I unconsciously think about it, but all I can think about to make me feel better is, "I'm still a virgin. Good."

I figured that maybe I'm a lesbian after all. Since being touched by a guy in a non-platonic manner grossed the hell out of me. I got close to this girl I considered a friend. I started to make friends with *actual girls* after that ordeal. What happened? What would usually happen when you hang out with girls, you get stabbed in the back. However, it wasn't just a girl, it was everyone I considered a "friend". My final months of middle school were lonely and my parents told me what they've told me all along: "Los amigos no existen. No puedes confiar en
ninguna persona."

Friends don't exist. You can't trust anyone.

I took that with me to high school. I started off as a cold kid. I wanted to do nothing with the other students, I wanted to study. I wanted to be as great a student as I was in sixth grade. I had no friends, but I was happy and intelligent. In case you're
wondering, "Why did you change?"

Bullying.

I was fat and nerdy, *of course* they'll pick on me. I was weak and kids are cruel, that why I became so butch in seventh grade. So no one can mess with me again. Funny how it all blew up in my face at the end of middle school huh?

Anyway, I inevitably, got close to these two girls I dub "The Twins". No matter how I pushed them away, they kept wanted to befriend me. Stupid me gave them a chance. I ended up talking to them all four years, but during senior year, we fought frequently. Not like guys, who take out their anger in one fistfight and everything is better, but the way girls would fight: either through a long course of sabotage, or a long, stretched out timeline of short arguments. Ours was the latter.

I got close to many people. Especially to this one tall, geeky, Jewish guy. I didn't like him at first because I was convinced that I liked his girlfriend, but the more I knew him, the more I thought he was a great guy. After that relationshit, I had a fear of men. Specifically, tall, white guys. This geeky guy fit the criteria. I spent a night at his house once when my mom was having were psychotic fits and believing everyone is turned against her. I was nervous, scared even. I remember I rested on his bed and he straddled me from behind. I freaked out, to say the least, but all he said was, "It's just me. Calm down."

All he did was give me a massage and set out a place for me to sleep on the floor.

This guy, was a genuinely good guy. To all you women who believe that all men are potential rapists are dead wrong. Nice, trusting guys exist and you're just paying too much attention to the jerks to see that.

Sure, he and I weren't best friends or anything, but I was no longer afraid of touch. Hell, if neither of us was attracted to the other, why should it matter? (I jokingly called him a "rapist" because he grabbed breasts and asses of every one he knew. Including other guys. Including me, but by that point, I was fine with it, it's just him.) Funnily enough, he kissed me one day. Like, the moment I walked in and said '*hi*', he grabbed me by the face and laid one on me. Why? I don't know, but I'm not ashamed to call that one "The best kiss I've gotten from a guy," compared to that atrocious previous experience I've had. I don't talk to him anymore, but I silently thank him for getting rid of my fear of men.

I got close to this other girl as well, she was cute, she was Asian, she was dorky and absolutely precious. I knew my boundaries with her the moment I met her. Somehow, in the middle of my high school career, I had openly expressed affection for the people I was closest to with hugs and kisses. I probably talked to her more than anyone else. Hell, people thought we were going out. Strangely enough, I felt nothing for her but a sisterly, protective feeling for her.

I met some other girls, growing somewhat less-misogynistic as I got to know them. Aggravatingly enough, they tried to get me a girlfriend. (I'm guessing because of this weird, borderline-lesbian *friendship* I had with this one girl.)

I toyed with the idea until I figured, 'Hey! I'm a lesbian, maybe I should try this dating this out!'

I didn't understand it at all. I mean, how can someone ask you out if you don't even know each other? Is there supposed to be this instant attraction? Is there a dating memo I'm not getting? It didn't work out, but I wasn't upset over it since I felt nothing for this girl to begin with. I was 17

at this point and I was starting to wonder, "What the hell is wrong with me?"

I went out with a few girls and it didn't work. I felt nothing. I kept trying because I wanted to feel that something that everyone is talking about. I felt this non-existent pressure, I *had* to find someone, I *had* to be in a relationship.

That was the year I learned about asexuality. I realized that I've never looked at someone and thought, '*Oh baby, I want me some of that! Bring it over here!*'

I can't see myself doing that. Man or woman. I can't imagine myself getting...err..*intimate* with them. So, that semblance of semi-normalcy? Thrown at the window. I was a high school student with no libido, no interest in love, nothing. I could at least have a best friend, right?

I fought with the twins. As time went by, everyone steadily grew distant, making false promises that they'll keep in contact once they were out of the hell-hole called "high school."

I never attended prom or graduation. Do I regret it? No. That cute little Asian girl even skipped prom to hang out with me and this other girl at Fanime, An anime convention. Time well-spent. You'd think that with someone like her, that we'd keep in touch, yeah?

No.

That's the funny thing about *friendship*. The way I see it, you're lucky if you hang out with the same people for all four years. However, once that object or person (in this case, the object being the school) that keeps you together is gone, all contact ceases. Once you're no longer forced to interact with each other on a daily basis, your so-called *friends* go away with it. The twins, made false promises to force me out of hiding to hang out with them, to be social. Let's say they broke that promise. They tried to get everyone together, but time has changed all of us. They're in college now, meeting and talking with new people. I'm still here, in my hole, hiding, unchanging minus the fact I grow steadily more cynical. Everyone simply grew distant and eventually forgot about one another.

Many disagree. My cousin is the type that believes that friendship lasts forever. To me, that's just as ridiculous as the notion of "soul mates". It's a childish idea and I believe that once you *really* understand people, you'll know that lifelong relationships aren't in their nature. It doesn't seem to be. They can hardly keep one mate for life, what makes you think they'll carry the same friend for just as long? I don't claim to understand them. However, from what I've seen and experienced, human beings are cold creatures.

I don't think I can ever truly understand people though, no matter how hard I try/tried. I can't understand their obsession with sex. I can't understand their need for companionship, for friendship. I can't understand how many expect to have a life partner or one friend for the remainder of their days and how they expect that to be possible. I can't understand the masks they wear, why they would act kindly towards one person, but say cruel things once that person is gone. I can't understand how people make promises that they have no intention of keeping.

This is why I have no friends, why I have no one to talk to. Why I can't get close to anyone, why I can't bring myself to truly care. Why I could never fit in with other people since day one.

Because for now and possibly for the longest time, I will *never* understand.

A Box, Potentially

SheepShot

"It is a very delicate contraption," Giuseppe said. "One gentle tip and it could all fall into pieces," he emphasized further as he examined the small box from under his magnifying monocle.

"But what does it do?" I asked inquisitively, as I looked at it, perched at the table, eyeing it with awe. "After all, it is just a box."

"You are forgetting that in a box, there is always something," he replied as he stretched his spine back into place. "This box, has the potential to do everything, because there could be absolutely anything inside it."

"But why is it so fragile?" I asked yet again, still not completely satisfied by what he had told me. "If it could do anything, why not make itself invincible!"

"It is not a matter of ability, it is a matter of potential! As it is, it is still a closed box. It can do nothing but break into my hands, rendering it useless. Though if you were to correctly tinker with it, you could create the best."

He turned round and started pacing, letting me flank him while still at the table looking at this golden box. "That box could be so much more, yet it is not. It'll probably be broken in the hands of an irresponsible teenager or a torn adult. It'll be misused and not given the respect it deserves. It'll be dismissed as simply a box."

"Then let us store it in a cupboard, high above the reach of all those who can abuse it!" I exclaimed happily, as I stood from the table. It was the solution. If you cannot touch something, you cannot destroy it.

He turned round, looked me in the eye and said "Alas, that is not a solution. If something is not used, it'll rust. And being destroyed is not much worse than rusting. No, the only solution is to let it bide, until in a moment of eureka we can open it, exposing it to the world. We will be hailed as heroes and saviours, until the Pandora element within is released, and we'll be viewed as nothing more than traitors and thieves. For we'll have stolen everything that was before, as we'll have unleashed something new."

"We'll have started a revolution. And people don't like change, unless it's contained in a fancy golden box."

To Pee Or Not To Pee

Graham Worthington

To pee, or not to pee – that is the question
Whether 'tis nobler in the mind to step
Out of the shower all soapy and wet
Or say 'fuck this, no one's watching'
And peeing on the floor, save precious time
That could be spent in viewing porn
This question – and a whole bunch more –
That people bug me with, I wish I could
Ignore. To pee, to smile, to gush and escape
The dumb opinions of others.
To pee: but there's a catch
For in that quick relief what else may come?
When I have thus let my sloth reign
What farts may press from my relaxed ass
And in their unchecked haste blast out
Turds long and brown and hideous
That I must snatch up in dismay
And juggling them in panic to the shitter
Risk slipping on the tiles, and by
So unwanted a fall, crush them to my
New-washed self, whilst through the door
My sister cries 'aren't you done yet?'
But that this thought has seized my mind
I would risk peeing in the shower
An untried pleasure, whose simple delight
No one I know will speak of
But rather do they glare, and loud insist
That only pigs pee in the shower
Thus conscience doth make cowards of us all
And thus the natural love of ease
Is screwed by the pale sneer of thought
And I do find I've lost the soap
And lost also in useless thought
Have peed unthinking in the shower

Roadlesstaken

Alex

I'm that spiky-haired, tennis-playing, daydreaming fella that's now a graduate student trying to figure out his future. I love seeing the world, interacting with a variety of people, and pondering about the experiences that life throws at me. "The sweet is never as sweet without the bitter," is one of my favorite quotes and it has helped me through some rough times. I have lived in Maryland all my life, but I'm planning on starting fresh somewhere else once I'm finish with my commitments. I'm a pragmatic optimist that hopes for good times ahead.

You Just Don't Expect it Sometimes

Roadlesstaken

The word "suicide" started popping up a lot today all of a sudden. Earlier today, I read a post by a Xangan which seemed like it was a suicide letter (hopefully, the worse case scenario doesn't happen). Later, while reading through a mail about life insurance, the very last bullet point under the *Information You Should Know* section read "Death by suicide in the first two years is not covered (1 year for Missouri residents)." Just now, I was hanging out with a friend when we started talking about the show House and how shocking it was when Kutner commited suicide on that show.

You know what makes this even more weird? I was actually in the process of writing about this topic for the past week or so, but held back because I wasn't sure what to say. I still really don't, but seeing as it's in my head today I'll write all that I can for now.

While in San Diego, I found out from my old high school friend that a mutual friend of ours passed away in March, supposedly from suicide. The thing that made this extremely shocking for me was that this friend was probably the last person I would ever think would do such a thing. She was one of those cheerful people that always smiles when she greets you (kind of like how I am). She was in the process of finishing up her masters and was at the time engaged as well, so those elements made this news even more boggling.

So what happened? There seemed to be no warning, i.e. note or change of behavior. What could have been so distraughtful to my friend that she chose this route, a route I would never have guessed? It's such a big difference from reading/studying suicide at school and actually experiencing the event in real life, that's for sure.

I still find myself experiencing all five stages of grief. I was in denial that such a thing could ever happen to my friend, one of the sweetest person I knew. I was angry that I didn't hear about this sooner, or else I would have loved to attend her funeral to pay my final respects. I found myself trying to bargain with God in my head, asking him if he could just send me back in time for a brief moment so I could try to talk her out of it. I felt sad of course that there was something in this world that can drive my friend down this unimaginable path.

I've more or less accepted it happened, as much as I really don't want to. I'm not walking around constantly distressed or anything, but I'm definitely still thinking about it. Whenever the topic of suicide comes up (as it has today), I find myself feeling just as shock and emotional as I was the first time I heard the news.

I really don't have any grand final thoughts on this topic yet. Perhaps I will revisit this later when I have it more figured out in my head. We'll see.

I miss you Tejal. Thank you for being a part of my life.

ReeserTheShadow

Reeser Winters

Reeser joined the Xanga community in December of 2005 and has enjoyed both posting and making friends ever since. In 2009, Reeser graduated with a BA in English Literature, and now uses it primarily to write poems riddled with monsters and short stories about what it's like to be a Goth. When not writing, Reeser enjoys reading (anything from Douglas Adams to Norse mythology or Anne Rice), attending Bible studies, volunteering at music festivals and local radio stations, and occasionally going out dressed as a vampire.

Are You Here to Worship?

ReeserTheShadow

"Are you here to worship the Lord?" David asks us. He's not Southern, but his voice is starting to get that way. "If you're here to worship him, then put your hands together! Give the Lord a hand!"

The people around me are clapping, and I clap a bit, too. It's difficult with the brace on my wrist. My left palm thuds dully against the fabric stretched over my right. I try to get into the clapping, but it hurts. Everyone around me keeps going long after I've stopped. Pink and yellow lights shine down on David's sweaty face. He looks like he could be made of glass, his skin is so shiny. He wipes his shirtsleeve across his eyes, and catches sight of me, not clapping. I wish I hadn't let people jostle me to the front of the crowd.

David clears his throat and takes up the mic again. I think I have offended him personally, as he keeps looking over in my direction. "Now, I don't know if you can feel it," he sounds like he's about to tell us a frightening secret—*don't move! There's a bear right behind you!*—"But I feel the *presence* of the Lord in this place tonight. We've got a real good message coming, but before we sit down, I want you to *worship*. I want you to *feel* the Lord's presence."

Please, please, please Lord—let my wrist stop hurting so that I can satisfy these people that my heart is in the right place... David should know my heart is in the right place though. He's only a few years older than I am, and his girlfriend is one of just ten other students in my year at our tiny Christian high school. I figure Erin must not talk about me very much or he would know better. David signals to the guitarist, and Colin starts plucking out a slow, sorrowful song.

Lord, why do they have to do things this way? Why, why, why do they think that playing this overly emotional music will get people to really *worship?*

David is about to start singing, but first he gives us instructions: "As we sing this song together, I want you all to lift your hands to the Lord. I want to see you show some lovin'. Don't you be worryin' about whoever's standin' next to you. What they think ain't so important as what the Lord thinks…"

Yeah, right it's not. I say a prayer for him: *Lord, please let David understand the words that are coming out of his mouth.* I try to stretch my arms up the way he's told us to, but just as my hands reach face level, I stop. There is a sharp pain in my right wrist. Slowly, I pull my hands back down, and the pain goes away. It's replaced with a burning sensation. My skin feels like it's itching from the inside. With folded arms, I pray for my tendonitis to go away, or to at least not drive me crazy. The itch is creeping up my arm, but I'm afraid to take the brace off and get at it. Wouldn't want the sound of Velcro to disturb anyone…

The song goes on forever. David looks over at me a few times, and finally I decide to just stare at the carpet. I close my eyes for good measure, since I knew that closed eyes would be equated with a deep prayer. Not that I wasn't praying. I prayed over and over: *Lord, why do I even come here anymore?*

My own youth group had been disbanded due to "lack of interest," so I'd accepted an invitation from another school friend, Kristen, to go to hers. For months I'd been showing up at the P— H— for youth group. It was nice to be around some people I knew at church, but everything was such a production. The music and the lighting and the inflections in the leader's voices were all designed to get you to think on your sins—think on the *looove* of *Jee*-sus!

Everything at P— H— was huge, too: the church, the parking lot, the lobby. The youth room was gigantic. Hundreds of teenagers could sit comfortably, or even stand all around the stage for parts of the service. It wasn't quite the same as my old youth group. Then, it had been a dozen or fewer of us, meeting in a mildewy basement to sing *a capella* and read from battered student Bibles under buzzing fluorescent lights.

Different physical spaces are easy to adjust to though. Culture shock is harder, and deep down, I knew I wasn't cut out to be Pentecostal. I just couldn't do it. Even before tendonitis had set in, I couldn't do it. Wasn't comfortable with the continual raising of hands. Not able to keep a beat, so I didn't clap during songs. Couldn't speak in tongues. *...Lord, why do I still come here?*

Finally, David's voice tapers down into sporadic "hallelujahs" and "thank you, Jesuses." I look back and see Pastor Debbie take up a mic.

"Yes, praise Jesus," I hope that she won't get emotional and start the music again. I don't think I can stand it. "Tonight we've got a guest. Sister Bear has been with us at P— H— for years, and she's such a dear soul. She's such a dear...she came to me and told me that she had a vision about the youth of this church," (here Debbie gets tearful) "about our youth falling into the hands of the Enemy, and I asked her to come and share it with you so that you can..."

I stop listening. It's never any good when a church person is talking directly to you, and yet they continually substitute "our youth" for the pronoun "you." I can't stand it. I can't stand being told that I'm "falling into the hands of the Enemy." Pastor Debbie says "Enemy" with a capital *E*. I can hear it in her voice, just like I can hear the capital *L* when David says "Lord."

Pastor Debbie allows us to go back to our seats. A few people are murmuring again, and I'm glad. The noise muffles the *chink, chink, chink* of the chains on my pants. They sound like the spurs of cowboy boots, right before their wearers get into a standoff.

I duck down into my maroon padded chair, and wonder who Sister Bear is. An image of an elderly biker-chick comes to mind: long grizzled hair tied back with a bandana, a leather jacket looking too bulky for an old woman's shoulders...when she spoke to us, it would be all fire and brimstone, and we would hear the husky evidence of her own smoking, rebellious youth. I know I am wrong before I even look up at the stage; Pastor Debbie would never bring someone like that to talk to us. No.

Instead, Sister Bear is a plump woman in an amorphous, flowered dress. Her hair is a faintly orange colour, bunched into a tight cap of curls on her round head. I can't quite make out her face because her glasses are enormous. As an elderly church lady, Sister Bear is unremarkable. I wonder if Bear is really her last name. I can't imagine that it's a nickname. Not for this woman.

"Thank you, Sister Deborah. I'm grateful for a chance to talk to our youth tonight." Her voice is very soft, her words shapeless as her dress. I suspect that Sister Bear never fully opens or shuts her mouth the way that most people do when they speak. What vision will be unfolded by this insubstantial voice? I'm mildly interested. It's not every day that you get to hear about visions.

"Hello," she says to the youth. And to me, I suppose. "I'm Sister Bear. As Sister Deborah mentioned, God gave me a vision about the youth here in this church, and I've felt it on my heart to tell you what God has to say." For a moment, I revel in being addressed directly. But, my revelry is short-lived: "God sent me a vision about Death. Death is coming for you, and you're letting her in."

I've been sitting in a careless attitude—one foot propped on the empty chair in front of me, my injured arm resting over the back of another empty chair to my right—and suddenly, I feel that this is wrong. I mustn't look like a careless youth, lest Sister Bear's bespectacled gaze land upon me. I've had enough of David getting it into his head that I'm not worshipping, and don't need an elderly Bear thinking I'm not listening to her, either. I sit up and fold my hands in my lap.

"My vision was of Death," she repeats. Good. I haven't missed anything. "And it was in this very room that Death was trying to get to you. In my vision, I was here—where I'm standing now—and I looked across the empty room to see that one of the back windows was open."

At this, several teens turn around in their seats to look at the windows. Most of them are sitting behind me, but I can hear their garments shifting as they twist around and whisper to their neighbors. Sister Bear starts up again.

"One of the windows was open, and as I watched, a woman started climbing in. I knew she was Death the moment I saw her, and I was terrified. I was frightened for you, our church's children!" Sister Bear sniffs loudly to show how afraid she was. "She was dressed all in black, Death, and she was so pale. When she got one leg over the windowsill, I could see she had pointed heels and those black, netted stockings..."

The attentive expression on my face is fixed now. I stare at Sister Bear without really seeing her. *So,* I think, *so, Death is a vamp. Death is a Gothic prostitute. That's great. That's just really great. Why does Death have to be Goth? When I get to heaven, I'm going to ask...*

I wonder where the other Goths, Danielle and Travis are—if they sense Sister Bear's vision leading up to a pronouncement on how we three dress. Not that Danielle and I are vamps. Still, I can only imagine who people's eyes are landing on when Sister Bear describes Death. How unfortunate that God sent Sister Bear such a *specific* vision of what Death would look like.

I try to listen again. Maybe Sister Bear isn't going to condemn the three of us for dressing like we do. Maybe, maybe: "...and when I saw that she couldn't come through the window, I pointed my finger at her and said, 'Death, you aren't wanted here! In the name of our Lord, I cast you out!' Death looked at me and laughed. She laughed and laughed, and she spoke to me. My dears, Death spoke to me, and do you know what she said? She told me that I could not cast her out because you had invited her in..."

I feel numb. *Lord, I hope that whoever is inviting Death in really gets something out of this message. All that I'm getting is that I'm not right for this church... I can't "worship" right, I can't pray right—I don't even* look *right!*

"...and then the vision of this room passed away and the Lord spoke to me. He said, 'go to Pastor Deborah and tell her that you have this message. Tell her that the youth need encouraged to seek the Holy Spirit's anointing'..."

Ah, I think, *so I must speak in tongues before I have any hope of casting off this so-called Death who is coming to drink my blood or whatever it was she told you she would do...*I try to stop my cynical line of thought and pray instead. *Lord, are you really going to let this Death come for me just because I couldn't lift my hands during the worship music? Is Tendonitis the forerunner of Death?* I pause before starting my prayer over. I'm sure God doesn't appreciate my sarcasm, even if he understands. *Lord, please let Sister Bear's vision be useful to someone here tonight. Please don't let people think that Travis and Danielle and I are evil because of it...*

The voice on the PA system changes, and I look up to see that David has taken up his mic again. "Sister Bear is right. In order to fight back against Death, we need to seek the

Holy Spirit! Why don't y'all come on up and we can call upon the Lord."

We all get up. I don't want to, and my feet drag. *Chink, chink, chink.* I'm a veritable Herald—capital *H*—of Death. What do I want to go up front for? Still, I allow the crowd to push me out of my seat and close to the stage. Now is a good time to go into "deep prayer" mode, and just wait it out. I feel very let-down by tonight's service. In spite of Kristen's assurances that her youth group wasn't judgmental, I feel unwanted.

I feel the tendonitis itching on the inside of my skin.

Very close to me is an outburst of glossolalia, and I can't help but glance over. I do a double take. There is Travis, after all. A knot of people surrounds him, laying hands on his black jacket and his shaggy hair. *All the better to pray for you, Gothling. All the better to get you to where we can think of you as one of us...*

I know Travis doesn't speak in tongues, but he's told me he wants to. I hope that he doesn't feel like it's a requirement for being a Christian. Hope he realizes that what God thinks is more important than what the leaders in this church think. Hope he doesn't feel like I do...

Travis is weeping, and I can't stand it anymore. I close my eyes and pray. I pray that the people who do speak in tongues will mean it. I pray that the people who can't won't be branded as particularly stubborn sinners. I pray for people to not hate Travis, Danielle, and I just because of how we dress.

I pray that I'll find a different youth group soon.

One Year Later

In memory of a great man

Vanessa E. Lord

He took the charm
From my open hand
With such reverence
For you, for me, and
For all that it meant
It was walking over coals
For the little boy-man.

I was giving the charm
To you, all over again
Hoping it would help you
Find your way to me and
Find all that it meant
It was cutting into my heart
And finding you there.

He stood straight and
Placed the charm
Close to his heart
He looked up at me
With your eyes, your smile
It was enchanting and I
Wanted to stay, falling.

Now it was my turn
To walk away, to walk on
With a bit of his heart that
Is a bit of your heart
That lives in my heart
Now *I* travel
Now *I* send the post cards
To one who could have been mine.

Memories of My Mother in Honor of Her Birthday

imTHEmeowMIXcat

Well, Mom got her flowers, she called me about an hour ago all emotional, haha…I'm glad she liked them. I was thinking of different things once I hung up. I realized that I have seen my Mom through so many phases.

I remember her from when she was going to Cosmetology school and she was practicing her skills on me. We lived at my Grandma's house then, Mom and Dad had separated. Not only did I accidentally drop one of her brushes behind the cupboard in the bathroom, but I insisted on making off with all of her polish sticker guides because they were silver, sparkly crescent shapes…and four year old me kinda had a thing for Star Trek.

I remember our movie nights, when we went back home to Dad and had our secret rules: while we had to eat like ladies at the dinner table like he insisted, it was ok to pig out on Sprees and Popcorn when it was "girl time." It was also ok to go out and get dirty in Grandma's garden. I will never forget the way the tomatoes tasted fresh off the vine with a sprinkling of salt. I love eating these on Summer days while I walked around barefoot in the mud of the shady walnut grove. Very refreshing.

She saved my teddy bear when some mean boy threw him over the fence of my preschool and into a pen with cows. I screamed with horror when I woke up from my nap and he was gone, and again when Mom came home after jumping the fence and retrieving him and his arm, which had been ripped off. She sewed him back together, gave him a wash, good as new. I had never been so relieved.

I will not ever forget the way she described heaven to me when I asked why Grandma had to die. She was so young, younger than I am now, and going through a divorce from my Dad at the same time. No wonder she told me years later about how lost she felt.

I remember her during her party girl stage, going to visit her and her roomate in their apartment, driving around town with her in her little red MR2. I was secretly amused by her permed hair that was crispy to the touch from all the hairspray in it and how she would dye her hair a new color every few weeks: dark, then bright red, then blonde. She and her roomate would watch the same workout videos over and over while I joined them in doing situps. I would curl my eyelashes while they put on way too much makeup to go out and my Dad would pick me up.

I remember when she met my step dad. She stayed up all night talking on the phone with him, drawing his name with little hearts around it. I drew mermaids and we watched Willy Wonka together religiously. I noticed I was spending less and less time with her.

I went to court with her once, soon after the divorce was finalized and Grandma was gone... Mom got a DWI. The Sheriff let me sit with him while she went up to the judge, I got a gold star sticker. Apparently she had tried to kill herself. I had no idea.

I remember when she stopped calling, she completely disappeared when my Dad went to college. I asked him where she went, he told me that she signed over full custody to him. I didn't understand what I did wrong.

She returned nearly a year later with a big surprise: A new husband and a beautiful baby brother for me. I couldn't have been happier. Seventeen months later, another little brother! I think it was then that I saw the "Mom" side of her, she had me so young, she didn't seem to know how to act like anything more than "big sister" to me. That hasn't changed. It was ok. It still is.

I think the best part about any relationship is seeing a person over time and appreciating their little changes. I think that that's one of the neatest things about having such young parents. I have literally grown up with them and I have seen them through so much. It hasn't been easy and there have been many many times I felt neglected, and angry...but that's the best part of any experience...being able to accept the bad and see the good anyway. I adore my Mother, and I really appreciate the kind protective friend she is now.

A Poet's Song

Andrew F. O'Hara

Many brave men lived before Agamemnon; but all are overwhelmed in eternal night, unwept, unknown, because they lack a sacred poet.

—Horace

"Pomes! All you know is your dumb-ass pomes!"

Arnie looked up in exasperation and closed his collection of Longfellow poetry. "Agnes," he pleaded, "I was just taking a breather from all the chores to sit back and relax for a moment with—"

"Them goddammed pomes!" Her hair still wild from the night's sleep, Agnes shoved and sent the vacuum cleaner rocketing across the floor to where Arnie sat. It slid to a halt in front of him.

"Them goddamned pomes are going to be the death of you, Arnold Grimsby! I don't give a big flyin' shit if you stay up all night, but we got stuff needs to be done and I'll be damned if you're gonna sit on yer ass and read and write stupid-ass POMES all day." She wiped her hands on her apron, turned her portly backside to him, and stormed back into the kitchen, muttering, "Goddamned pomes. What'd I ever do?"

Arnie sighed and tucked his book safely under the recliner. He grasped the vacuum cleaner. Flipping the switch, he absent mindedly began sliding it across the carpet. "Shhhh-waaaa-shhhhh-waaa"...the sound of the vacuum began to lull him, and he improvised a melody with a background of "shhhhh-waaaaah—shh—"

"You silly son of a bitch, if you keep doing the same spot long enough, there won't be no carpet left!" She yanked the vacuum from his hands. "Get your ass outside and get to work on that fence before you forget how to do it. Get out—hear me? Out!"

The pile of fresh boards for the new fence was, indeed, waiting for him as he stepped out into the heat and found his hammer. He had cemented the last post in place yesterday and put up the skeleton framing.

He squinted into the sky. The blistering sun of the Sacramento Valley was merciless to those who showed it no respect. He would work more slowly than yesterday, when he'd gotten dizzy in the dry wind and taken refuge under a stream of water from the garden hose. Not good, not good, for a man his age.

He grabbed the first board and steadied it against the frame. With several nails drooping from his mouth, he tacked it up and stepped back.

The nails and hammering squeezed the pine juice from the board, and when the smell reached his nose he remembered his young days as a forestry worker high in the Sierra Nevada Mountains. Pine needles and sunlight still streamed in his memory through a cloud of limbs overhead as his feet sank in a cushion of moss and mulch. Arnie paused, smiling, and began composing a poem in his mind.

A smell of pine that lingers in your nose
and sap that sticks to your fingers,
clinging desperately to days past,
to days long gone...

"Listen, dickhead, if you like, I'll take one of them boards and shove it up your ass if that's what it takes to get the work done around here!"

Arnie jumped and looked around. He hadn't heard the window open or seen Agnes glaring at him. He snatched another board and hastily hammered it into place.

The morning passed miserably as Arnie worked on the fence. Once, he slipped into the house for a glass of water and ice; he couldn't see her, but he knew Agnes was somewhere, her "radar" tracking his every move. Quickly, he guzzled his water and fled back into the mid-day summer heat.

Bam, bam, bam. Grabbing the next board, he held it in place with one hand, pulled a nail from his mouth and hammered it in.

The sun began slipping from its zenith and toppled toward the west, but the heat for the next few hours was still unrelenting. Arnie paused from time to time to wipe his face with a bandanna—and moved on to the next section of fence before Agnes heard the pause.

Arnie groaned with exhaustion and finally squeezed against the house for what little shade was left. There remained only a few feet of fence to complete, he noted. There would be plenty of time to finish it in the morning before the heat set in.

Pulling a stick of chewing gum from his pocket, he peeled away the damp wrapping and popped it into his mouth.

Arnie remembered when life had been better, sweeter. That was a long time ago. A younger, prettier Agnes had delighted in his poems. During their courtship, she had sat under the pines and by the streams and giggled as he had weaved and spun words to tickle her imagination.

It had been a delightful romance, so many years ago. She'd loved his romantic side; that part that seemed to fly in the clouds with such ease, murmuring of strange and beautiful places and kings and their queens and streams that bubbled with magical sounds that only he seemed able to translate into words that broke their meaning.

The death of their only child had embittered her. She had blamed him because, he being a forester, they had lived so far from the hospital and been snowed in. She had refused to try for another child. With each year, other misfortunes of life had beaten his wife into unyielding steel, leaving her a woman whose every word was a comment on the hopelessness of even staying alive.

Though they had found a nice little home on a hill in Redding after his retirement, she stayed bitter. It always puzzled Arnie that he had managed to remain so much the same, in spite of Agnes. Perhaps, he thought, it was because he'd clung to his world of poetry and found refuge in it at the worst of times. Often, he'd tried to share this same comfort with Agnes, reading to her in soothing tones. She'd jump up angrily and drown him out with the television.

Arnie had given up sharing his inner world and now just tried to find it in secretive places and times. He'd keep a solemn face, yet celebrate inside when Agnes left for a card party or a shopping trip down the valley to Sacramento. Then, he would race up to his study, prop open the door so he could hear her return, and eagerly open one of his treasured books. Occasionally, he'd become so engrossed in his reading that he'd miss the sound of her car pulling in. Startled by the hollering and doors slamming, he'd race to hide all evidence of his crimes before she marched up the stairs.

Grabbing a mop or dust rag, he'd smile innocently, heart racing, and stutter, "I was doing a few things to surprise you!"

She'd peer around suspiciously and grunt, "Humph," then storm back down the stairs.

The golden times of his life were when she left for a night or several days to visit friends or relatives. With hours on his hands, Arnie would grab whatever writing paper was available. He'd charge up to the desk in his study on the second floor of the house. Using these precious hours of freedom, he'd sit and write his own poetry, hands shaking with delight and words spinning out so fast that he'd get confused and throw sheets aside in frustration.

Such opportunities were rare.

At dinners, Agnes was merciless in haranguing Arnie in front of guests. She could render any dish tasteless as she launched into her favorite subject in front of company.

"We went on a cruise to Mexico," she would begin. "You know what eight-ball here brings along? A tuxedo? No, he forgets that. He brings along a suitcase full of his pome books! Thinks he's gonna waste his cruise money sitting up on the deck staring at girls and reading all these pomes to anyone that'll listen."

"Can you *imagine*?"

Crowing, Agnes would continue as their company fidgeted nervously.

"People thanked their lucky stars for me, I guarantee you, because as soon as I saw what he was up to, I snatched them books and started throwing them over the side, one by one, right there in front of him and everyone. Yes sir, was a good thing I was there."

Looking over the unfinished fence, Arnie wiped the sweat off his brow and sighed. No matter. Years had passed and he had learned to take what pleasures he could get at the times he could get them. A breeze blew along the side of the house, announcing the approach of evening.

Laying down the hammer and wiping his eyes, Arnie opened the door and slipped into the house. Somewhere, in the back, he could hear Agnes running water into a bucket and muttering about "dirty windows." Stealthily, he slipped around the corner of the dining room, down the hall and tiptoed up the stairs to his study. Quietly, he closed and locked the door.

Rarely did he dare lock it but, Agnes being in the house, he didn't want to risk her catching him writing. If she pounded on the door, he would have time to hide his hand-written sheets, casually unlock the door, and swear he'd been taking a nap. She'd be skeptical but would probably accept it with a few quick curses about taking a nap while she slaved.

Arnie seated himself at the desk in front of the window and, spreading out a blank piece of paper, looked out at the view.

The shadows were settling into the yard and the only direct sunlight was touching the tops of the highest trees, painting them a brilliant yellow. Arnie loved this view from the second floor. In the distance, a haze had colored the mountain range a strange pastel of grayish blue. The snow-capped peak of Mount Shasta loomed high on the horizon. As his mind relaxed, Arnie remembered a poem by Longfellow:

> *I can see the shadowy lines of its trees,*
> *And catch, in sudden gleams,*
> *The sheen of the far-surrounding seas,*
> *And islands that were the Hesperides*
> *Of all my boyish dreams.*
> *It murmurs and whispers still:*

A boy's will is the wind's will,
And the thoughts of youth are long, long thoughts.

Arnie smiled at the mythical Hesperides Islands with trees that bore golden apples. The quiet of the summer afternoon played on his imagination. Unable to resist the urge, he picked up his pencil and scooted his chair under the desk, writing and pausing only to glance out the window at the scenery.

The crash of an aluminum ladder startled him and he dropped the pencil. With a clattering bounce, the ladder came to rest against the sill of the window from which he was looking.

There was a heavy clambering of feet and Arnie was suddenly staring directly into his wife's hostile eyes.

Holding a squeegee and water bucket in one hand, she tore the screen off and began clawing at the window's edge to open it. Her mouth was already moving but the sound was muffled by the glass. Without thinking, Arnie rose and slid open the window.

"—leave me to take care of these goddamned windows by myself while you sit on your ass and write your weirdo pomes. Well, I'll tell you, you worthless sack of shit, I didn't climb all the way up here to watch you get away with that! NOW I know what the hell you do up here. When I get in there, you'd better get out of my way, you dildo, because I'm gonna burn everything you have in there!"

Arnie sighed. He leaned across the desk and gave the ladder a push.

It was quiet for a long time, except for the sound of Arnie's pencil on the paper. Assured of quiet, he picked up the telephone.

The Courtyard

Graham Worthington

A courtyard, stones laid to form an enclosed square. It lies by the holy temple, and will fall into the temple's shadow, but now the sun stands high and the square is bathed in sunlight.

The dancers take their places, facing each other in lines, each dressed as best they can afford, each as erect as they can hold their untamed flesh.

Oh accept me, do not reject me, I extend my arms in love, will you blast me with your scorn?

And they advance, each hand whipping ribbons, tight clenched in fear, stepping left and right stamping in defiance.

By the holy temple, soon to be in its soothing shadow, by the sunlit square.

Will you match your steps to mine, will your eyes meet mine? You are fair my slender partner, will you fire my rising heat? I am bold, but my step trembles, will you mix your heat with mine?

And they advance, and they withdraw, and their steps smite the hard stone.

See my ribbons, see me flash them, red, green white and sky mocking blue.

Do you love them, do you love me? Will you quench me O my partner, will you quench my rising heat?

In the bright square, by the holy temple, not yet shaded from Apollo's blinding heat.

Oh I desire you, oh I cannot endure without you, why did I enter this dreaded dance? Yet dance I must, and I compel me, and you compel me. Leave me, love me, oh do not leave me.

Joy! I cannot endure such joy. Oh let the holy temple cast its merciful shadow.

By the holy temple, in the sun bright square.

We face each other triumphant. We step, the music obeys us. And I and you are the holy temple, and we are the sun bright square. Let me hold you, let me enfold you, and when our fires mix to an unendurable heat, let us forget the holy temple, yet cry with grateful tears for the cool of its advancing shadow.

What is up with Asian Women?

verified-but-still-denied

By writing this article, I already know that I have warranted my death sentence. Therefore, I have drafted my will and left it at an undisclosed location. However, this is a dire issue that needs to be discussed about and brought to people's attention; where death is but a small sacrifice for the benefit of Mankind.

What the Hell is up with Asian woman? Like every woman, they will never come to admit their faults, let alone acknowledge it. The Asian woman, ESPECIALLY in America, is one of the most indecisive, hypocritical, elitist, extreme, narcissistic, manipulative creatures on the face of the planet. You Asian female readers can deny this all you want, but I only speak the truth through observation and experience. I realize that these characteristics can be applied to all women but Asian women have managed to find a way to make their own case in these extremes. Here is how I'm going to start off.

They are NEVER satisfied with anything you do. As a boyfriend, friend, or person. There is always something you did wrong and not up to standards with them. You can build the Eiffel tower for them and they will tell you that it's nice but you forgot to put a screw in one of the 7 million holes. Normal women are very appreciative and will be grateful and pleased when someone gives them a gift of some sort and will show at least a sign of appreciation. However for Asian women, there is always something wrong with what you're giving them. "It's too cheap", "This other girl's boyfriend does this....", "Well he does this...." etc. There is something they can always do better or something they forgot to do. And even if the male actually, for once, did things up to par, you probably have bent over backwards and stuck your head between your legs, only to get a less than enthusiastic and fake-ish "thank you". Anything and everything can be underappreciated according to Asian women. This of course brings up the next issue with Asian women.

Asian women are extremely unreasonable. "EXTREME" is the key word in this situation. How so? They will and have always been something of an anomaly. They will want the nicest guy with all the characteristics of a Disney prince. However, in addition to that Disney prince, characteristics of asshole-ism and douche-bag-gery have to be thrown into the mix too. The Disney prince at most times are supposed to emulate the knight in shining armor; the selfless, the romantic, the loyal, and devoted icon and dream man of women everywhere; is not enough for Asian women. To them, those characteristics are nice to have, and are quite desired, don't get me wrong, but they want their boys to have a bit of "Greaser" (cultural reference to the movie "Grease") in them too. The dream male for them is a combination of oil and water. Something that should NOT go together for the fact that the two zones would always be conflicting. In the likely situation that they will not find that guy, they will go and find the bad guy first and save the prince for marriage. After going through 5+ bad boys first. However, if they do find that guy, it's not enough. Why? They want more, and they know they will get it.

Maybe this characteristic is in all women, but what I have noticed is that Asian women are probably the most manipulative people on the planet. These ladies are not stupid. They know they have characteristics that only THEY have. They know who to target and how to target them. Whether they are the boys with yellow fever, or the people who are suckers for their "innocent" charm, or people who would succumb to their "adorable" voices and smiles. THEY KNOW HOW TO HUNT. Watch closely and carefully of how they get people to do what they want for them. They will completely change themselves and will do every little thing to lull you in, and as you come in closer thinking they are nothing but harmless little girls who just want a moment of your time, they clutch you in their grasps and you become their slaves for the rest of time (or just for the time being they need you). All that charm that suckered you in the first place? Gone. How come? Because you're too busy scrubbing their floors to look or hear that charm that you fell for in the first place. The moment you realize that you fell for it and try to make a run for it, they immediately go back into succubus mode and charm you back into doing their work until it's done.

This is just a small side observation of a significant amount of Asian women. Has anyone noticed that they seem to be the least proud of their heritage? It may take a while to see it but if you look around, you may notice that there are a good few who try their very best to dissociate themselves with Asians or as an Asian. There is absolutely nothing wrong with hanging out with people of other races, as a matter a fact I encourage it, but these girls refuse to try and be friendly or refer themselves to anyone that is of the Asian descent. In certain instances they will go around saying "Psh. I'm not Asian you fool. I'm *enter another race here*. So don't call me Asian. Ha Ha Ha.". I think it's perfectly fine to find interest and embrace other cultures, but to deny your own birth right? I think that's pushing it a little far. This doesn't go to all Asian women, but it's something I've noticed about a big amount of Asian women in general.

These are just a few of my findings on Asian woman and their flaws. These women, who do so much harm; from the emasculation of men, transforming once good men into the bitter, miserable, angry assholes. There is no end to their destruction. So to every male out there, beware of the Asian female, for they are like a game of Russian roulette. A high risk game with high risk rewards but can ensure certain death of your life, soul, or character once you lose.

SerenaDante

Smaranda

....is 20 years old and studies at McGill University in Montreal. Though her studies have often taken precedence over other things, writing has always been her greatest passion, especially writing fantasy. It took her seven years to finish her first novel, Courage of Story, but she hopes to write more very soon. Especially, she enjoys writing short fantasy stories.

The Dazzling Fairy Ball

SerenaDante

The splendiferous annual fairy ball took place on a spellbinding evening at the palace of the sublime emperor and empress of fairies. All fairies of even the slightest importance manifested themselves in the enormous ballroom of the palace; every bogie and elf and imp, every pixie and gnome and dwarf, every nisse and every nymph appeared in full regalia. It was a battle royal to see who the most magnificently decorated fairy there was; and every hope, every wish that evening was to be that one that none could lift their eyes from. As the sirens coquettishly fluttered their eyelashes, wearing hardly more than the waters of their lakes, the empyrean angels illuminated the ballroom wherever they chose to float. As the statuesque elves blatantly flaunted their archery skills, the hags, the only completely banausic fairies, paraded into the ballroom.

And there, in a brilliantly arranged corner of the ballroom, sat a ridiculously royal cat named Eleanor with her ridiculously loyal boyfriend named Armand, discussing the fairy turnout of that year.

"That pixie there looks like a dumpling in that dress. What *was* she thinking! And there, that siren, oh *look* at her flirting away with that elf, a pure temptress! I hope he doesn't like her very much at all! This is not a very dazzling ball," said Eleanor. The elf and siren left together that moment, looking rather friendlier than she had hoped.

"Well put," said Armand, as sycophantically as possible. He wanted to be on her good side that night, if any such existed, for he had a certain question he wished to ask her momentarily, and he wished to receive at least a relatively positive answer.

In any normal conversation, feline or otherwise, a silence of any length should have ensued after the last comment. It did not. Eleanor gave a half-smile at the fawning compliment as she continued to speak: "And the angels! Ugh, they're far too bright; it's as if they've brought the moon, the stars, *and* the sun this time! It's quite painful to the eyes. This is *not* a dazzling ball at all!"

"Yes, darling, very true. Now, El," said Armand. "I'd like to ask you a question."

"Hmm? Of course." She paused just long enough for him to gather the last bit of courage he needed; but just as the words were forming in his mouth, just as his lips were preparing to open, she launched into another bout of complaints. "And the hags, oh dearest moon, the hags. Why *must* they come to the ball? They spoil everything, *really* they do. All this beauty, this color, and then them. This is *not* a dazzling ball at all anymore! Why does the emperor even allow them to be fairies anymore? It's not like they're anything *really* special."

"Love, I doubt that's the emperor's choice. They still have plenty of magic. Now, I have something very important I absolutely *must* say," said Armand. He nervously felt the beautiful diamond-studded collar that he was hiding under his paws. "Darling..."

She paid no attention, for now something new had distracted her. An animal nymph had entered, shadowed by a radiant leopard with flaming orange fur. "Oh my, now *that* is something worthy of this ball! I must go introduce myself...I wonder if that pretty little nymph would be willing to give him up to the emperor's own fat cat?" She raced over to the leopard as Armand looked forlornly down at the collar, then back up at her.

She was prancing in front of the leopard, as seductively as a fat cat could prance. He was being completely unresponsive. At last she stopped, and said something that immediately caused the leopard's eyes to become engrossed. He looked up at the nymph as though asking permission, and Armand realized that the nymph was not his girlfriend. With a sinking feeling in his stomach, he watched Eleanor and the leopard dance once, closely, and then a second time, even more closely. At last Eleanor seemed to notice Armand, still stretched out on her pearled and sequined and feathered pillows. With an air of hauteur she walked towards him. Armand held his breath. "Darling..." he began softly, as she stiffly sat down in front of him.

"Please don't darling me," she said coldly, then embarked upon a hackneyed, memorized speech. "I'm afraid I must break off our relationship. Whatever you have found in or received from this, you may keep, except for my heart, because that now belongs to another. We can no longer have any contact whatsoever. Is that clear?" She did not wait for an answer, but muttering to herself, she sauntered away. Armand thought he heard her saying something about wearing a diamond-studded collar to impress the tangerine cat – a diamond-studded collar that she had recently purchased at the price of several hundred thousand pieces of gold.

Armand looked at the remarkable collar he had hidden under his paws, not in any particular shock, and airily finished the sentence he had tried to start several times. "Darling, I found your collar on the ground – might I wear it?" With a giggle, the charming cat strode away from the corner, dimly aware that he was now among the richest, and certainly the most gorgeous, felines alive.

It had been a dazzling fairy ball.

Waiting

Shards_of_Beauty

Waiting

Dancing under a blood red sky
Crackling flames pile high
Casting demons in relief on the ground
Choking gray hatred drifted thick
Falling ashes crush air
Damping spirits breath no sound
Stumbling over black rock earth
Scraping bone bare mirth
Waiting fire to rush and surround
Waiting
Running
Burning

Burning
    Melting
        Sinking
           Falling
Pressure
    Weight
        Time
          Darkness
Crying
   Moving
       Waiting
         Breaking
Broken
   Chipped
       Watched
         Used
Catching
    Reflecting
        Shining
          Waiting
Carbon
    Fire
   Light
                  Diamond

mizz_chan

Ally Chan

I love writing and have always found it useful as a means of escape. I started writing in seventh grade and haven't turned back since. I am currently a student and I aspire to be a teacher. I want to teach kindergarten because I think that it's really important to instil a love for learning in young children at an early age. We can only have hope in our future if we trust that they understand and appreciate the importance of education not only in school, but as a life-long process. I love travelling and hope to travel and teach when I am finished school. My xanga is a mish-mash of my writing other the years – anything and everything that's come to mind.

Happiness in Our Hardships

mizz_chan

It was the perfect summer day. The sky was the perfect shade of blue and not a single cloud littered the sky. A slight breeze ran through the house, creating the perfect temperature. Our minds rested as we curled up under the covers to take a break from the sweltering heat outside. We jolted awake to the shrill ring of the telephone and my cousin jumped to get it.

It was our parents; we knew this for sure. We had been awaiting their call from the hospital. My grandma had gone in for a surgery. The doctors said that it would be minor. Our parents let us take the afternoon off to rest and they stayed to wait there. They had promised to call once it was finished. I watched and waited patiently on the bed while my cousin spoke with my aunt. I watched her expression change and the tears forming and falling from her eyes. She hung up the phone and I immediately asked what happened.

"She had cancer. The doctors said she has at most six months," whispered my cousin.

My mind raced. The questions came pouring into my head. What happened to minor surgery? Why me? Why her? I was scared. We both collapsed onto the bed in a heap, holding one another and crying. We let the tears flow and comforted one another, telling each other everything would be okay. We both knew however, that things were more uncertain then than they had ever been.

We finally composed ourselves and got in the car to drive to the hospital. It was still perfect outside. The sky was still blue, the air hot, the breeze fresh and crisp. As I sat and watched the world go by through my rolled-down passenger side window, I wondered how the world could keep on going as if nothing had changed. My world had just been flipped upside down and yet the outer environment had not altered an inch.

The next few months consisted of juggling school and hospital visits. In November, my grandmother was well enough to move to a nursing home. It was there that she spent the next seven months. Throughout this time, friends and family from all over came to visit. The love and joy that surrounded her was undeniable. Her room was constantly filled with warmth and laughter. Even through her sickness and pain she persevered. She never once showed us the full extent of the pain she was suffering. Instead, she brought us closer together as a family and created some of the best memories we have had with her and with each other. Even though she is now gone, her love and memory still lingers. We were blessed with not six, but ten long months to say our final goodbyes and those ten months were nothing short of wonderful.

carolinavenger

Sara Urban

I am a reader, a writer, and a super hero. I know 380 digits of pi, and am hopelessly in love with everything I cannot have. I'm so adjective, I verb nouns. That's all there is to say, really.

The Um-Friend

Carolinavenger

*an um-friend is a term coined by a friend of mine. It is the stage between a friendship and a relationship where you are introducing the other person to someone and say this is ----------, my, um... friend.

He bursts into her apartment at nine. Without a word he goes into her room, pulls an emerald dress from her closet, and throws it and a pair of patent leather heels into her lap on top of the open book she holds. I'm not letting you sit here on a Saturday night alone, he says. You can read any night. Not tonight. Get up. Get dressed. Out we go.

She takes a moment to recover from the blast of his intrusion; his shockwaves still buffet against the living room walls. She tilts her head just a touch to the side and blinks a few times, her face a blank, considering what ought to be done. She does not in fact have any desire to leave her book or her cushy plaid sofa, but she has also never had any success in the past trying to convince him of this. Having as yet said nothing, she closes her Vonnegut, gathers the dress and shoes, and pads on bare feet back to her room to change.

That's my girl, he says.

She stands at the end of the bar nursing a strong gin and tonic, trying to remain invisible to the Jersey Shore lookalikes, watching him parade about on the dance floor like a peacock. His dancing is exaggerated tonight and he is making something of an ass of himself, judging by the faces of the girls nearby. She smiles inwardly for a moment because something tells her he is doing it on purpose and no one knows except for her. She then quickly dodges to the side as a girl too drunk to handle stilettos any longer nearly topples into her. Whatever is left of what the drunkenness was drinking is now trickling down her calf. She scowls. No one notices.

He pushes through the crowd to find her. There is a brief break in the music while the DJ makes an announcement. Do you want to dance? he asks.

She shakes her head no. I don't dance, she says.

Why not?

Long story.

Are you having a good time?

She hesitates. Yes, she says.

Are you lying to me?

Maybe. The music starts again.

Well what's the matter then?

She scans the room as best she can, considering the erratic flashing of colored lights. I don't like all these shallow drunk people, she says. I don't like this music, at all. And I especially don't like HAVING TO SHOUT OVER THE MUSIC TO TALK.

He studies her face while she contemplates the dregs of her drink. Her shoulders heave a sigh. She looks profoundly sad. You can stay if you want, she says. I'm going home.

The door of the bar bangs shut behind her. As she begins the eight-block trek homeward, she hears it bang again. She turns around. He has followed her out.

What's wrong? He asks.

I told you, in there.

You don't like bars?

I don't like bars that try to pretend they're nightclubs. I don't mind quiet bars, but those are usually full of alcoholic old men and that's just depressing.

Well if you don't like them, why did you come out?

She folds her arms across her chest. Her jaw clenches and her eyes look at something off to the side that isn't there. Because you told me to, she says.

You could have said no.

No I couldn't have.

Well of course you *could* have. I mean, I realize I was kind of insistent about it, but you could have told me to eff off, get lost, something. You tell Jake that all the time.

That's the point you're missing, she says, biting her lower lip for a second. I couldn't because it was you who asked. I can't say no to you.

What? Why not?

She looks into his warm amber eyes and says nothing. A minute of silence passes, broken only by the sound of rubber against damp pavement as a solitary car slowly explores the quiet side street they are on.

Her eyes drop to the sidewalk. I'm sorry, she says. I know I'm no fun.

He closes the six-foot gap between them in two steps and pulls her in close. That isn't true, he says. That isn't true.

He pulls away after a few seconds and puts a finger to her chin, tilting her face upward till she meets his gaze. You wanna get some ice cream?

The ice cream place is open until midnight during the hot part of the year. They make it with four minutes to spare and split a dish of mint chocolate swirl covered in chocolate sprinkles. They sit at one of the tables outside, watching the boy who served them wiping the counter and counting out the money in the register through the window. A small speaker above the window pipes soft classical music into the humid night air.

As she scrapes the last spoonful from the bottom of the dish she says, Actually, I lied earlier. I do dance, sometimes.

Really?

Yes. She points to the speaker with her plastic spoon. Real dancing. Waltzing.

I can't say I've ever waltzed before, he says.

She pushes back from the table, stands and offers her hands to him. Would you like to learn?

As the boy who served the ice cream finishes putting away dishes and returns to the storefront to lock up, he hears a commotion outside his window. STEP-two-three, STEP-two-three. No, like this. Listen to the music. Ouch, my toe! And he watches as the boy picks up the girl by her waist and spins her around and around while she wraps her arms around his neck, laughing.

They burst together through the apartment door in a mock tango. He twirls her around four times until she finally breaks away and stumbles into the hallway. Stop, I'm getting dizzy! she protests.

He fake-ballets past her and takes the first right into her bedroom, tossing himself facedown onto the length of the bed and moaning into the pillow. He's been doing this since college, since the first day he sat on her bed and found out her mattress was the most comfortable in their dorm and then made every excuse to nap on it when she wasn't there.

She stands in the doorway, left hand on her hip. Okay, smart guy, she says as she slips out of her heels and tosses them, one at a time, back into the closet. Where am I supposed to sit, then?

He rolls over on his back, moving to the side of the bed bordering the window, and pats the empty space beside him. She sits down gingerly, parallel to him, and pulls her knees up to her chin.

Now what? she asks.

Well I don't know about you, he says, but I'm exhausted, and I'm going to sleep. He turns onto his side, facing the window.

On my bed, she says. Nothing ever changes. Why don't you go back to your own apartment?

Your bed is much more comfortable.

Well where am I supposed to sleep then?

Shhhhh.

She is very close to grabbing his ankles and dragging him off the bed. She's done it before. She did it in college probably once a week. She gets up as if to do so and he grabs her favorite blanket from the foot of the bed and covers himself with it, as though it will protect him.

She stands on the hardwood floor and looks out the open venetian blinds, at the town made yellow by the sodium streetlights. She walks out to the living room and turns off all her own lights. She hits the wall switch as she returns to her room, lit now only by the dim yellow stripes which fall across the bed. She wriggles out of her dress and quickly pulls on an old cotton nightgown that had been hanging from the foot of the bed, then slips under the blanket and cuddles up to him. She has never been a big spoon before; in fact she has never been a spoon at all. Interesting, this silverware business, she thinks.

What's this? he mumbles half-coherently, bending his legs a bit so her knees can fit behind his.

She puts an arm over him, across his chest. Shhhhh, she says.

He moves his own arm over hers, linking their fingers together. That's my girl.

She listens as his breathing becomes steadier, then slower. When she is sure he is asleep she moves closer, until the tip of her nose is touching his shoulder blade, and breathes him in. She watches through the blinds the absolute stillness of the town and is content.

Pane

Scott Christian

She dances along a pane of glass
Wild and free
She has no set direction
Nor bonds to hold her back
She leaves a trail
behind her -- where she's been
I try to imagine her life before
A feat
Impossible

The sky beats a dull colour
it's grim sheen cast upon
my face
I hear the gentle rap upon my roof
The patter of countless trails
to follow
I smile -- faint, obscure
We've danced this step
before

I place my finger
to follow the trail she left
I dance to her steps
jagged -- but beautiful
And as she slips below the line
I stop for a moment
in mournful reflection
I slowly place my finger
upon another trail
And I think to myself
"Maybe, this time
she'll stay?"

Ghost Boy

Alyxandri

Alexis lies awake in the dark. It is four in the morning. She hears a faint rustling noise and flips on a light. There, standing in front of her closed bedroom door is the young boy. He is solid, then he fades. He shimmers. He stares. With his blue eyes, he stares.

Alexis sits up in bed. She stares back at the boy. She slaps herself across the face, hard. The boy blinks.

"You are still here," Alexis says.

"I'm always here," the ghost boy answers. There is static in the background of his voice. "The signal is good tonight."

Alexis runs her fingers through her hair. Her eyes dart from side to side, up the walls, up to the ceiling, always coming back to rest on the boy. He stands still and stares. Fade in, fade out.

"I don't want you here," Alexis says abruptly. "Get out. Get out! Now. I don't want you here! Get *out*!" Her voice is shrill, hysterical.

The boy turns toward the door. He reaches out a translucent hand.

"Wait. Stop. Stop, please. Please, stop. I didn't mean it. Please, don't go. Don't leave. Don't leave me alone."

The boy turns around. He stares at her tearstained face. In one fluid movement, the fluid movement of a child, he sits cross-legged on the floor facing her. He folds his hands under his chin and looks at her speculatively.

"I didn't hurt you, did I?" Alexis says.

"What's to hurt?" The boy replies. Pause.

"You weren't really going to leave, were you?"

"I can't. You've locked me in."

"I didn't do that."

"Then who?"

Victory

Graham Worthington

The soaring eagle, in yearning flight

Spends all its days to buy the far horizon

Though all broad flapping of its wings

Halts not the sun's relentless course

Nor stays night's final victory

Its bones will lie on some tomorrow's hill

Grey, half hidden in the dingy turf

And rot beside the dead sheep's corpse

But now the sky is blue, the white clouds pure

And from the dizzy height it sneers down

To where earth's weighty crawlers plod

Blinking dull eyes in useless envy

The moment is victory, free of care

And all else but a dismal dream

Blood: My Fascination

Breaking_expectations

I'm not scared of blood, in fact, I'm captivated by it.

Being prone to nosebleeds, blood was something I had a lot of exposure to at a young age. I loved the deep red colour. I loved the taste. I loved the way it splattered all over. I loved blood. When my nose would start to bleed, my classmates would freak out. Some of them would even cry. The normal reaction to blood is horror, for it is so often connected to pain and suffering. Blood has always captivated me, as twisted as that sounds. Aside from the simple captivation I have with blood, I love the symbolism and effect that can be created through blood.

Most people connect blood to death, but blood can also symbolize life. It's pulsing through the veins of every living person, it is essential. The increased heart rate caused by caffeine consumption, athletics, being close to someone you're attracted to, adrenaline and being in danger, pushes the blood faster and faster through the individual. These things can be felt throughout the body, creating an amazing effect. This is feeling alive.

Blood also represents truth, for it is one of the few things that cannot be altered. In the superficial society in which we live, people are always trying to change themselves and hide who they are. Blood is the very core of a person, a part of them that they cannot change to fit society's standards. Unlike the external body, there is no form of hair dye or plastic surgery that can modify the substance flowing through one's veins.

The bond between family members is described by the words "blood relatives." This emphasizes the true connection, wanted or not, between people who happen to come from the same family. As much as I hate to admit it, I have my father's blood running through my veins. I would love to say that I hold no connection to him, but that would be a lie. Biologically, I hold a lot of the same genes he does. Heritage is also emphasized by blood. It is seen as a point of pride, being able to claim that you are tied by blood to a certain country or group of people. *(On a side note: did you see the Norwegian curling team's pants? I'm so proud to be partially Norwegian, just for that.*

A lot of people think it is twisted to actually like blood and find beauty in it, but I think blood is one of the simplest yet most complex representations of human life. There are so many different ways one could interpret it, but this versatile nature is just another aspect of humanity one can infer. Aside from all that though, just the look it has and the way it tastes, I'm strange but I like it.

Do you like symbolism? What does blood symbolize to you? Do you find beauty in unconventional things?

Jaynebug

Lyne Hamel

Perspective. Perspective. Perspective. Life is full of them and I find myself intrigued on a daily basis. My "slice of life" and inspirational writing gets its life from my everyday adventures on the central coast of California. I have been writing on Xanga since January of 2009, and the experience has been a journey all its own. Xanga has provided me a place to write and along the way I've found myself in the flow toward my best self. When we put our thoughts, feelings, ideas, and emotions in this space, we are taking that step to connect to something larger. (Pats heart and points to you.)

Blessings

Lyne Hamel

The first time I saw her must have been after we moved out of the canyon into town.

"What was that?" My eye caught movement on the corner as I turned right.

"What was what Mommy?"

"I thought I saw somebody standing there throwing something. Maybe they're just talking with their hands. It just looked strange."

"It was a lady, Mom. I saw her. She's moving her mouth and there's no one else with her. She was moving her hands. Who is she Mom?"

"I don't know, Honey. I only saw her out of the corner of my eye as I turned back there," I said looking over my shoulder. "I hope she's okay."

The next time I saw her, I was at another intersection. As I took the right hand turn, there she was. There was a bike next to her, and she was making the sign of the cross and her mouth was moving in what I thought was probably prayer. Then as I drove pass, I realized she was blessing each car and it's occupants as they passed by her at this busy intersection.

"There's that lady, Mom," my son said from his seat in the back.

"Yes. I saw her."

"What is she doing?"

"I think she's blessing people."

"Blessing people?"

"Yes. Um... she is sending them a thought, a prayer for maybe safety or finding goodness in them. A blessing."

About a month later, we were in a different section of town and my son saw her first.

"There's the Blessing Lady!"

"Oh. Yes. There she is."

"Do you think she's blessing us?

"Yes, I do. I think that's sweet and thoughtful of her. What do you think?"

"Do you think she's crazy?

"What do you think?"

"I'm not sure."

"She looks like she's quite content to just be doing her blessing thing, Honey. That doesn't make her crazy."

"That makes her nice?"

"That makes her special."

We'd see her then she'd disappear for a few months, then there she'd be again. We'd unroll our window and wave at her. My son started saying; "Thank you for the blessing" as we'd roll by. She never stopped her work, but her expression was of kindness and an inner joy filled her face. I felt blessed every time, so her work was working at least in my willing corner.

She had a bike by her side for years. Then we noticed she had a wheelchair and she was in the same place for a while probably due to having to wheel it herself. That bike had kept her in shape and her blessing meter of giving most likely helped hold her up. Then we saw that she had a motorized wheelchair and we knew she'd be getting around to other corners again. She did.

Once when my husband was in the car we saw her. My son asked him if he thought she was crazy to do "that" all the time.

Just because she's sitting on the corner blessing people doesn't make her crazy son. Maybe that's her work here on earth. Is she bringing any harm to others?"

"No, but don't you think it's strange she's been doing that for all these years?"

"It's her choice, and I'd like to think she's doing a kind thing for our area. She's adding some positive energy to a busy, crazy world. How could that be wrong?"

"Yea....I feel kind of good after I see her Dad. I've been seeing her since I was about four. Remember the first time we saw her, Mom? She sort of freaked us out, then we got use to seeing her and we were happy when we did. She's part of my childhood memories now."

My husband looked at him with immense love in his eyes. "That doesn't sound crazy to me."